So, I had a Thought

Nigel Derbyshire

Carbon Writer

So, I had a Thought
by Nigel Derbyshire

Copyright ©2021 by Nigel Derbyshire

All rights reserved. This book or any portion thereof may not be reproduced or used in any manner whatsoever without the express permission of the author except for the use of brief quotations in a book review or scholarly journal.

First Edition: June 2021

ISBN 978-1-9164156-3-8

Publisher
Carbon Writer
carbonwriter.net
publisher@carbonwriter.net

Dedication

To Amy & Oliver, a constant source of inspiration & hope.

Acknowledgement

People need to be acknowledged, for their help in creating this.

Unfortunately, I wasn't keeping a list of those people, so this will be rather on the short side.

I would like to thank myself, for allowing me to write this.

Contents

Setting the Scene   1

<u>CLOSED THINKING</u>   5

on-off Tribalism
   - Our predisposition with binary boxes, will destroy us   7

Debate
   - Stop the doom, by talking more & shouting less   13

Noise Disappearance
   - An aspiration of Noise Disappearance?   17

Finishers & Completionists will kill us all
   - World-sized problems, need reckless folk   23

Beige Rectangles
   - Latch and follow, is less than ideal   29

CONSTRUCTIVE THINKING 33

Warning Lights
- Driving an old car, will help you fight fake-news 35

Journey; semi-colon
- The existence of the semi-colon is proof 41

Time
- We have the wrong type of time 45

Trying to remember
- It's all specifically sketchy 51

The wrong way
- Perspective is everything 59

Stressful Calm
- It's not the thing, it's the control of the thing 65

The Words of Movies
- Self-regulated joy 71

Connections
- Joining the dots from A to unknown 77

Episode v Season
- Perspective is more than you think 83

Einstein's Weather
- It's all about boats and twigs 89

Effort v Effort
 - It's all about amount and location 93

The Longhand World
 - Old maps and pencils, will improve your world 99

<u>CREATIVE THINKING</u> 105

Creative Place
 - You need to find your creative place 107

Cracks in Reality
 - All the stuff in-between 113

I have no idea what I'm doing
 - I really don't 117

Just Thinking
 - Have you ever wondered, what it was like 123

Collecting
 - It's not about the doing 129

The Language of Words
 - Your self-representation 133

Glue
 - It's more than you think it is 139

Scrolling Entertainment
 - A meander through cheese, pickled onions & electronic glass 145

WHIMSICAL THINKING 153

Magical Pie
- We need to talk about pie 155

English Breakfast
- Its omnipresence, is a lesson for us all 159

Words are a funny ole thing
- I am just leasing these words from the language 165

The Jelly & Marshmallow Wars
- The untold buttery war 171

The Gibberish of Rhubarb
- The long game 177

A Conclusion 185

No one is looking; no one is listening
- Create with abandonment, not with measurement 187

Bibliography 193

About the author 199

Setting the Scene

We all have a need to think. To think about when we want a cup of tea, to think about what's for dinner, to think about what to watch on TV tonight. We think without actually thinking about it.

There are those of us, where a thought can veer off the road onto the grassy verge of worry, then sometimes into the ditch of despair. Then of course, we see the light-heartedness of the ponder. You may ponder a whimsical notion of changing the dining room wall colour. Or indeed, about spending fictional money on a fictional car that you could drive to a fictional home.

It's all good stuff; it oils our minds.

There is though, a gap in all of that. Or perhaps a missing something or other, that nourishes our minds. It's something that we don't often stumble upon, during our busy lives.

I'm talking about *active thinking*, or maybe *pro-active thinking* better describes it.

It is the action of taking a moment, taking a notion or idea and actively perusing it in your mind. Giving yourself permission to explore it. To muse over it. To apply some pro-active thought to it.

Why is it important? I think of it as a form of mental exercise. Just as taking a brisk walk helps improve our body, so a brisk stroll along a path edged with ideas and notions, is equally as good for our minds. That's not all, having an exercised and well oiled thinking brain, will give us better tools to be able to navigate the information rich world that we live in.

By way of example, I've done just that here. Some are entertaining, others thought provoking. I've loosely grouped them into, closed thinking, constructive thinking, creative thinking and whimsical thinking. Read them in any order, it really doesn't matter; there is a table of contents to help you navigate. They will perhaps, give you a jumping off point for your own thinking journey.

My call to arms is quite simple. To feel better,

to have better brain-tools, to give yourself a head start in tackling the information overloaded world you find yourself in.

Read the words, take a moment, have the thought, start the journey.

Closed Thinking

It's something that we have all encountered, closed thinking.

Not always obvious to spot at the time, often easier in hindsight, but closed thinking can be difficult to counter. In my experience, there are two distinct types; pro-active & passive.

Passive closed thinkers often just have a restricted view of matters, or just don't consider the notion that there are other possibilities. Through conversation, those are easiest to engage with. Sometimes, you can be surprised to find that they actually have the more enlightened position, and that it is yourself that has a closed view. Engaging with these folk can be rewarding.

Pro-active closed thinkers are another matter entirely. These have an enforced, or intention-

Closed

ally obtuse, view of the matter. Their default position is that everyone else has to be wrong, because quite simply they are correct. This self-belief can vary from being annoying, to being deliberately destructive. It is one thing to have that as a viewpoint, it is quite something else to force that onto others.

To be clear, I'm not saying that my position on any matter is better than others. No, not that. I do though, hope that I can engage in a respectful conversion with others whom I differ.

Over the next few chapters, I've pondered closed thinking. What it is, and what I view as the potential consequences.

on-off Tribalism

Our predisposition with binary boxes, will destroy us.

The other day, I walked into a dark room. I fumbled for the light switch, and then it wasn't. Dark, I mean; it was still a room. That, dear readers, is what we are talking about here.

As you imagine it, you will see it in two states. Dark then Light. It is a simple visual idea.

Now, let's take another example; coffee. How do you like it? With or without milk/cream? Again, another clear idea. What about tea? This time, the item is sugar; with or without?

Before you get into a panic, this is not a test and I won't be checking up on you at the end.

2+2 = 4 is right; 2+2 = 5 is wrong. Fire is hot; ice is cold.

I think you probably get the idea now. It is the idea of binary, or duality.

There is a whole junk load of stuff that our brains insist in categorising into binary results. We seem to like the on-off, true-false, yes-no, outcomes. Which is, kind of odd. I mean, we don't think of numbers like that?

Our view of numbers is influenced by the number of fingers we have, 10. When we get to 10, we just add one to the most significant digit and repeat. When we think about language, in English, we have 26 letters in the alphabet. Sure, others have more but the point is, it's most definitely more than 2.

Why then, with our language and number systems being most definitely more than 2, do we often prefer outcomes that are neatly categorised into 2?

I'm not a philosopher, but it is something that I do find slightly curious.

Someone once said that you can divide the whole of the United Kingdom into, Tea with, and Tea without. Sugar being the 'with'. Over 100 million cups of Tea[1] are consumed *every single day* in the United Kingdom; that is quite a large sample size!

However, as I am sure you have deduced, this is not the entire picture. Yes, I like sugar in my Tea, but sometimes I like 2. When I walk into a dark room, and make it less-dark, sometimes I like a dimmable light.

An espresso is milk free, but a latte has lots of milk and a flat-white also has milk, just less of it.

It is not a yes-no answer, it is more granular. It is closer to the number or language systems of assessment.

OK, so you get what I am talking about, but why is this a problem? Why does it matter if "Tea with" has a number of possible answers?

It actually does matter, quite a lot.

For reasons that I can't quite seem to fathom, there is a trend to want to resolve questions into this binary response-state. When understanding, or assessing answers to problems, we appear to be more comfortable in a yes-no, for-against, win-loose, pattern.

I've got a hunch that it is somehow linked to how we consume such question-answer narratives.

If we go back to the 19th century and look at how these sorts of things were discovered and read, when you had to look at the newspapers. You would see they were verbose, and the conclusions were just as verbose. No chatty snippets to be found.

If you look to the current, and at something like twitter, then the questions only have 240 characters to squeeze into, as does the answer. The nuanced answer about you preferring latte on a Tuesday because that's when you go to the gym and it feels like a reward, but how you like espresso on a Saturday because it helps with the night-after feeling... well there just isn't space. You are forced into a response that has to be yes-no.

I'm not blaming twitter for this. It is also linked to how rapid we need to consume the vast amount of news and information that is presented to us. We have to scroll through an epically large, and ever growing, catalogue of news and information. If we don't, then it either builds up, or we will miss out on something; it all has to be bite-sized.

So, why does this matter?

It matters because we are all missing out on the wonderfully complex and nuanced answers to simple questions. We are missing out on the *some-*

on-off Tribalism

thing that makes us human. It is not about yes-no, it is a glorious kaleidoscope of possible answers.

It is more though. It can result in something else. It can force people into tribes of yes-no, or loose-win, or with-or-without. This enforced tribalism creates conflict. You have these clans of people who will only accept binary absolutes.

All of the subtleties of responses, of outcomes, are lost in this binary state. A binary state that has become the default of our times. We need to make a change. We need to accept that more complex answers are not a bad thing. We need to embrace people who are in-between, on the fence, rather than shoehorn them into one camp or another.

Until we address this problem, the really big problems that face us on a global scale, will remain impossible to resolve. For a numerically & linguistically complex group, it really would be tragic if we ended up destroying ourselves because we were forced to think about things in such a binary way.

Closed

Debate

Stop the doom, by talking more & shouting less.

It seems that the art of debate has been lost. We should all be concerned about that.

You only need to take a look at the state of the current political landscape, to see how the art has been totally lost. In a few short years, we have gone from debate, to argument, to shouting.

There are of course, extremes in all of this, but I am talking about the mainstream. Different people have different political ideologies; something that used to be allowed. In the current climate, there is a trend of assuming that *I am right and you are wrong.* Which soon migrates to, *you shouldn't even be allowed to say that.*

It is certainly true that in politics, robust argument and even shouting, have always been part. However, those events used to be somewhat short-lived and focused. In the United States, regarding Donald Trump, and in the United Kingdom, with Brexit, it has been constant for multiple years. The fallout of that is having a profound effect on our larger society.

As onlookers, we regularly see individuals on both sides of the argument, loose their temper and descend into almost shouting. Whilst one could say it has some entertainment value, it actually demonstrates a distinct lack of skill and imagination.

In a political setting, there is something called debate. It works by letting your opponent state their case, to which you then attempt to deconstruct it or highlight flaws in it, whilst also expressing your alternative view regarding the same topic. Or, you attempt to derail them into talking about a topic that you feel more comfortable with.

It can be forceful at times, but the basis of the debate is to out manoeuvre your opponent, using your debating skill.

Those debating skills appear to be shockingly scarce in present times. Worse, they seem to have been replaced by something more sinister.

The approach used to be something along the lines of ... *"I know you are wrong, and I will demonstrate why my view is right."*

Which has now moved to ... *"Your view is wrong, and I'm going to show others how wrong you are."*

Then ... *"You are so wrong that it should be obvious to everyone how wrong and stupid you are."*

To ... *"You are so wrong, that it is offensive to me, and should be to others."*

Then predictably ... *"Your offensive ideals shouldn't be allowed to exist."*

Of course, the person on the other end of this, feels the need to get equally combative, and likewise will soon turn to mirroring the same line of attack.

Why does this matter?

It matters, because we soon end up in an emotive state of groups of people shouting about what they *don't want*, whilst devoting less and less time expressing what they *do want*.

Furthermore, that negative thought-loop starts to leak out into the wider community, away from politics. People then start to mirror that behaviour, and start creating mental lists of things (or people) that they don't like. Rather than thinking about the things they do like, and thinking about how they can get more of the things they like.

This leads to intolerance, which leads to extremism, which never leads to anything good.

The current clumsy & sloppy kind of tribal argument, that we are all witnessing, results in less new ideas. It results in large groups of society shouting at one and other about all the stuff they hate.

This creates the perfect setting for extremist groups to grow and prosper, as history has shown time and time again.

We do not need to be merely tolerant of other views, and ignore them. No, we need to engage with them, and find ways to debate with them in a way that illuminates an alternative view, rather than just attacking their view.

In doing so, those illuminated views may well foster ideas, which will in turn help resolve some of the overwhelming problems that face us all.

Noise Disappearance

An aspiration of Noise Disappearance?

The other day, I had to get my iPhone screen fixed. It was coming up to the 2 year anniversary, and I remembered I had paid for AppleCare. So, I looked at the "local" Apple Stores, and determined that whilst the Cambridge store was certainly in a delightful setting, it would require me to take a bus into the centre so that I didn't have to pay the stinging parking fees. So, I chose to drive to Milton Keynes, only 31 direct miles away, to visit the Apple Store there.

It was typically raining, but in a half-arsed kind of way. You know, that way where your windscreen wipers can't decide which mode to go in to; casual, or manic. 65 minutes of driving later, with a disproportional amount of parking-stress at its conclusion, I was there.

In contrast to my local Cambridge alternative, Milton Keynes is a "new" town. By that, I mean it seems like it was essentially designed in a few meetings, rather than over several hundred years. Yes, I know that I am over simplifying this, but you maybe get the point. It is a perfectly acceptable clinical execution of what a city would look like if it was designed and build in the last 50 years, or so.

OK, let me just come out and say it; Milton Keynes has the sense of being "over designed". I expect that for some of you that is a good thing, but I'm not in that particular Venn[2] diagram intersection. I'm not saying that there is anything wrong with Milton Keynes, but in my view it doesn't have the same texture as Cambridge.

Anyway, I rocked up to the shopping centre, then subsequently to the Apple Store, and duefully deposited my iPhone to them. As expected, the service was faultless, and the conclusion was as expected; nothing to see here.

However, there was a gap of an hour or so, where I had nothing to do. It was then that something started to unsettle me. It took a moment to work it out, but then it struck me. It struck me in a subtly annoying way; piped music.

To be clear, it wasn't the actual music that was being played. No, it was the fact that someone decided that music needed to be played at all. I was in a shopping centre, a mall.

To appease my step-count, I ambled around and spotted no end of specifically placed speakers for piping the said music into the ambient setting. This was not by accident; it was by actual design.

Why the music, what are they afraid of?

I found somewhere to sit down; I'd done enough of those steps. I took a moment to view the vista before me. The brightly coloured shop fronts, the tall ceilings looking down onto the marble floor. The people, a mixture of those rushing about and those ambling along. What would happen to these people if the music just stopped? Would there be mass hysteria? Perhaps the music is designed to take the edge off the shopping experience? You know, like a shot of vodka before an interview.

The music was metaphorically and actually, noise.

It got me thinking, what other kinds of noise do we have in our lives, and is it getting louder?

Closed

When I look at my Facebook feed, it feels like there is more re-sharing of stuff than there used to be. Perhaps it is just the mix of people that I now follow, but compared to my memory of it a few years ago, there are less original posts. It's tricky to quantify though.

Twitter feels like that too. The cliche of people tweeting about every mouthful of food, or just even waking up, seems to have gone. Again, that is only a feeling. So, I decided to put some numbers around it.

For something quite unrelated, I had collected some data of 6.6 million tweets. So, I did some quick analysis as to the number of retweets (the noise) verses the non-retweets (the original content). I have to say, I was a little shocked;

Out of 6.6 million tweets; retweets = 4.5 million (68%) original = 2.1 million (32%)

My feeling was true, two thirds of what is whizzing around twitter is noise; a non-scientific approximation, but it does give an indication.

With piped music, constant re-sharing of content online, there is more noise in our lives than ever before. It feels like a problem to me. Think about how much brain power we waste filtering out the noise from the original content.

Noise Disappearance

It's feels like trying to read poetry, whilst someone shouts at you. If the noise disappeared, I do wonder what we could all do with that extra two thirds of our minds...

Closed

Finishers & Completionists will kill us all

World-sized problems, need reckless folk.

We all know at least one. The person who is full of joy at finishing something. The person who gets immense satisfaction in finding all the flag-things in that game.

I present the Finisher & the Completionist.

For both of them, it is the conclusion of the exercise, that makes it all worthwhile.

If we take a moment to look at the Completionist. The term originates from the world of gaming. It is a specific category of person, who exhibits a

Closed

desire or obsession, in completing every aspect of a game. It can apply to any type of game, or indeed, activity.

As an example, we could take the game Animal Crossing: New Leaf, on the Nintendo 3DS handheld. I'm sure you won't be surprised to learn, there is a website that details for all games, the time taken to complete them. They have multiple definitions of *complete*; Main, Leisurely, Completionist. With increasing amounts of time. In the case of Animal Cross, the Completionist time is 1109 hours. Yes, eleven-hundred and nine hours, of continuous effort.

Put another way ... 1109 hours, at 1 hour per day, say during your lunch break. That is 5 days per week, with lets say 2 weeks off for a vacation; 250 hours per year. Yep, that will take you 4 years 5 months and 7 days. That is, of course assuming that you don't get distracted during your lunch break, by that argument between Tracey and Sharon in Accounts.

There are also, of course, the Finishers. Those strange folk who get enjoyment in concluding a task or project. For them, it is all about the finality of it.

In the workplace, Finishers tend to get more

recognition and reward.. There is a notoriety in finishing a project. A special kind of badge that is given, either figuratively or actually, to those special folk.

A niche exists with Finishers as well. They are called the Speed Runners. Their focus and laser sighted goal, is to complete a game in the shortest possible time. The record for Animal Crossing: New Leaf, is an amazing 1 hour 27 minutes and 15 seconds. It really is a sight to behold!

I am none of those people.

I am as far away from those people as it is possible to get; we will get onto that later.

Having observed such strange folk from a distance, I have noticed a number of curious things. The first of which, that just by looking at them, it's not possible to deduce which people suffer from this affliction. Secondly, said people will tend to focus on the *finishing-value* of any given task.

This is natural, and is a consequence of the task-reward loop that exists in most of us.

The consequence of this, appears to be that when given a task they will be more willing to start one when they can determine that it has a conclusion. Furthermore, those tasks which they know *how* to complete, will be given special favour.

Back to me. As I have disclosed, I am not any of these. I am best described as a *Startist*.

I have a fantastic ability to Start anything. I can pick up any task, I can start almost anything. I can get things going. I have no interest at all, in the *joy* of finishing something.

In our social structure, I do not get any kind of reward for Starting something. Indeed, it is frowned upon.

To be clear, I am happy to start anything, even those problems/tasks that do not seem to have any possible conclusion or solution whatsoever.

Why does this all matter; what has this go to do with anything?

Well, if we are to have a task-reward system that favours those who complete things, and which effectively penalises those who are good at starting, we will end up with less of the latter. We will end up with less Startists.

I've mentioned elsewhere[i], that I believe that our future holds a number of really difficult problems that need to be solved. Surely, we need to, as

---

[i] See, *Debate; on-off Tribalism.*

a group, work together to attempt to solve these problems. However, if a junk load of people are Finishers, then their focus is on the potential solution *before they have started*.

It's a problem. It's a problem because it is an immediate barrier for *trying things out*. What we need are those wonderful people who are fantastic at *Starting anything* without any kind of knowledge/will/desire in the conclusion of it.

We not only need ideas, but we need people who are willing to try everything. Once things progress past that initial stage, and fall into a plausible position, then the Finishers can take over.

If we are to solve these world-sized problems, we need a happy band of reckless folk, who are front-line Startists.

My name is Nigel Derbyshire, and I am a Startist.

Closed

Beige Rectangles

Latch and follow, is less than ideal.

I didn't use to have a phone. It took a good few years for me to get one. I just couldn't see why you would want to pro-actively talk to people. I have though, had a *Personal Digital Assistant* (PDA) since the early '90s. I liked the separation of duties between the two. The PDA was about information. The phone was about communication.

This separation meant that each class of product was free to express itself in whatever design language it chose. Choosing a phone in the late '90s and early '00s, was a delightfully diverse experience. It wasn't just about the features that were present, it was also about the look and feel. It wasn't even down to the company that created them, since product lines themselves would be

Closed

massively varied.

My preference seemed to have been Nokia, although I do admit to being diverted to the Motorola Razr V3i[3] for a while, Designed like a Star Trek communicator, the design was and is still, iconic.

Nokia too had their design delights. The Nokia 7280[4] being of particular note. It was designed to look like a flattened lipstick or perhaps a perfume dispenser. It had a small screen, which faded to a mirror when off, to allow you to check your makeup. It had a small camera, but had no keyboard at all. Instead just a tiny wheel was all you had. Listed by Fortune magazine as one of the best products, in 2004, and won design awards in 2005; this was and still is a highly desirable design marvel.

There was choice in the extreme.

Now look at the current mobile device market. Rectangles.

We all get excited about an improved camera, on the rectangle. Or the screen, on a rectangle. Or the flashy colours, of the rectangle.

There has been such a convergence of design, and indeed of feature-sets, that everything has turned into a vanilla-black beige landscape.

This tendency is everywhere. A race to be more like the perceived leader in the field.

Whilst there are outliers, such as Nintendo with its Switch, it just doesn't feel like there are enough.

I'm not saying that these products are *bad*, I mean it is great that I can instantly look up who was in a particular movie right from the palm of my hand. I guess I'm saying that the design-language has become a little stale.

So, why does this matter?

As I stated in *Finishers & Completionists will kill us all*[ii], the lack of original and diverse ideas, will be the undoing of us.

I think we can see it in how people act, or react, to situations. I'm not sure what it is called, but it feels like a herd of animals, being directed or coerced from one side of the field to the other. I would say, who decided that we were in a field in the first place?

There is a tendency to locate the perceived *ideal* and to then latch onto it. Be it a philosophical

---

[ii] See, *Finishers & Completionists will kill us all*.

ideal, or a physical ideal. This latch-and-follow approach, is worrying.

We certainly need that kind of behaviour, it can be a fantastically good thing, and is surely a requirement of a health society. But it shouldn't be the only thing.

Being different, is not a cool thing. Sure, being different is a cool fashion statement, but it feels like having a group of different people, is less acceptable than previously. Maybe I've got that entirely wrong. But as I wrote in *on-off tribalism*[iii], the desire for categorisation is a bad thing.

There is a default position of *suspicion* to those who do not neatly fit into a box, rather than an acceptance.

I'm not saying that all forms of *different-ness* are good, rather that they are in general given a lower *status* than the herd.

This might be how society actually works, and I'm just seeing more of it because of the ease in which it can be exposed and displayed.

Then again, this might be the undoing of us all.

[iii] See, *on-off Tribalism*.

Constructive Thinking

It's not all about being closed or creative. Sometimes it is better to just think about things in a more constructive, or pragmatic, way.

I often find myself pondering the possibilities of something. The notion of meandering along a thought-filled pathway, just to see where it goes.

These next chapters are my efforts in trying to take a notion, and turn it into something that could loosely be construed as *constructive*.

Constructive

Warning Lights

Driving an old car, will help you fight fake-news.

OK, so I drive a kind of old car. It's not a classic car, but it has done over 175,000 miles. It's a 2008 Mercedes E-Class. It has lovely comfy seats, and is designed to transport you vast distances without fuss.

Anyway, whilst the engine is just bedding in - I have been told more than once that it is good for 400,000 miles - the other aspects of the car have, *coughs*, character.

Over the last year, I've had a variety of warning lights appear on the dash. I think of it as *warning-light-bingo*. My strategy of late is based on one of pragmatic reality; I'm a poet and author, I have no money, so I will just ignore them.

Constructive

Sure, sometimes it is just helpfully telling me that I need to fill up the washer fluid, which I usually get around to. Oh, while I think about it, please please *please* can car makers tell me this when I start the car, and not after 15 minutes, as I hack down the fast lane and an almost legal speed!

Back to my point. I have noticed a couple of things. I find the usual warning lights, a greeting of a kind. It feels like the car is saying "Hi, good afternoon." Which has the rather curious effect of me not wanting to "fix" them; it would detract from the car's personality.

Now let's be clear here, the car is totally safe, and we are talking about superficial issues... almost. I mean the brake system failure warning light, is actually a failure of the sensor rather than the entire system itself. Albeit, if the brake system did fail, then the cute little light wouldn't help me. To be fair, I would most likely notice the failure, as I applied pressure to the brake pedal, only to be presented with nothing; the light wouldn't fix that, just give me notice of the impending doom...

The other day whilst driving, a new light appeared. It was the doom-ladened Yellow-Triangle punctuated with a (!). I was on a motorway at the time, so I approach it with the importance that it warranted. I ignored it, on the basis that it was only yellow and not red.

After a few miles, it was followed with further messages stating that the, EPS (traction / stability control), Cruise Control, Speedtronic, and Tyre Pressure, systems were also non-functioning. I accordingly (marginally) reduced my speed, and ambled home.

As I sat on the driveway, looking at the multi-coloured dashboard before me, I took a moment to think; was it time to part ways with this car? That thought made me sad. Having driven over 100,000 miles in this car, I had a "relationship"with it. No, I concluded, that relationship deserved slightly more than a dismissive gesture. (This obviously had *nothing* to do with the fact that I had no financial means to replace/fix the car...!)

My approach was two pronged. 1, How serious was the actual problem? 2, How difficult / costly was it to fix?

After some online sleuthing, I determined that the systems that failed were all inter-related, which explained the multiple messages. The cause of the fault seemed to swing wildly from "just a sensor", to "just a sensor that was a nasty pain in the arse to replace".

Constructive

My mood changed from mild-anxiety-induced panic, to mild-anxiety-induced indifference; it wasn't life threatening.

So, just like the brake-system warning light failure, the thing that had broken / switched off, was a driver-aid. It was something that was designed to protect me from my idiot self... that got me thinking.

My first car had nothing like these systems. If you drove like an idiot, then you would crash (like an idiot). My current car (pre-fault) would allow me to pull out of a junction on a wet slippery road, press my right foot into the floor, and it would "take care of things" for me. It was essentially "idiot proof".

My point after a rather over-long pre-able; is "idiot proof" a good idea?

To be sure, there are certainly a number of idiots who would be well served in being protected from themselves, but what about the rest of us?

When I drove my first car, I was acutely aware of my surroundings and the road conditions. Sure, I couldn't always do much about the aquaplaning or the sudden black ice, but at least I was connected to it. I had an appreciation of the limitations of grip that the car & tyres could provide. Now, I am entirely disconnected from it; I am electronically protected from the reality of my surroundings.

If we take a wider view of this, and look at the trend of protectionism and snowflake-ism, it is by some measure a safer place. We are protected from our idiot selves. However, we also have less "contact" with the reality of the world.

Does this matter, if we are "safer"?

It matters because we are loosing a vital skill. I'm not just talking about understanding how the laws of physics apply to a moving car. I am talking about our ability to discern idiots and junk, on the Internet and in real life.

We certainly need to protect certain people, who were certainly previously left (unreasonably) to fend for themselves. However, in our attempt to do that, we often blanket-protected everyone.

In doing so, we may have indirectly removed a vital skill; to effectively identify and handle idiots and mis-information....

For me, it turns out that I am actually quite OK driving around with those cute lights on the dashboard.

Constructive

Journey; semi-colon

The existence of the semi-colon is proof.

As I go through life, sometimes running, sometimes sitting, sometimes falling, sometimes climbing, there is a sense that you just need to do *enough*. There is that underlying trend that whilst you need to do your best, it is also perfectly OK to do *enough*.

Generally I have found that this is linked to the idea that life is full of destinations. It is full of places to get to, either physically, emotionally, or mentally. It is a series of points. Get to and through them, and you are making progress. Granted, sometimes we go backwards, but that is OK too. You just need to know where the next point is, and head towards it.

Constructive

Look at the modern techie world, and you see that people are executing on this big time. They are rushing to the next point, the next tweet, the next snapchat thing, the next high score. A massive series of points that need to be visited and ticked off.

In 1494 Italian printer Aldus Manutius[5] created the semicolon,[6] with Ben Jonson,[7] being the first English writer to use it systematically decades later. It can be used to link related clauses. It can also be thought of as a pause longer than a comma, but not quite a full stop. You don't have to use it at all. It is not like a full stop, that always needs to be used. It is not like a comma, which you can use to add some pause and tone to the written sentence; it is something different.

The semi-colon is something that doesn't really need to exist. Its usage has also declined in recent decades too, from a peak in the 1800s.

In a world of destinations, in a world of full-stops and commas, what does the semi-colon say about it all?

It is a powerful reminder of something so important, and defines a fundamental human trait. *Journey.*

There is a tremendous pressure to get to the

next point, to get to the next event, to get the next best grades, to be next, or to be first. There is a focus on full-stops. The commas are only there to let you plan, to briefly pause, so that you can get to the next full-stop more efficiently.

The semi-colon doesn't help with any of that. It does nothing but add noise. It is rubbish and has no place here. It is still here though, you still see it kicking around. So, why am I talking about this?

The semi-colon reminds us that the word-journey and sentence landscape is just as important as the concluding marks. In fact, you can't just throw a semi-colon into a sentence, like you can with a comma; thought is needed.

You need to plan for a semi-colon, you need to appreciate the sentence, the tone and the style. It needs to be worked into the sentence to make it work. Adding a semi-colon can elevate a mundane sentence into something special; semi-colons add value.

Semi-colons teach us that for some the journey of a sentence is just as important as the contents of the sentence, and more important than the destination.

We still use them now, some 500 years later.

Constructive

How has something that is so 'odd' still managed to stick around? Could it be that it is an example that shows, although we are currently focused on commas and full-stops, that we are at heart more of a journey people.

Despite what we are currently being programmed for, at our core we are all about *the journey*.

Travel defines us as a race, and the semi-colon is the literary from of that.

If you want proof of that, you have just followed a word journey this far, on the promise that I will explain the value of the semi-colon.

Time

We have the wrong type of time.

It's a funny old thing. Sometimes there is too much of it, sometimes there is not enough of it. It seems to be somehow elastic.

Don't worry, this isn't going to turn into an essay about General Relativity. Although that would actually be interesting (for me) - But, it's not about me, it's about you.

Actually, this is about me, this is all about me, but I understand that I need you to make it all about me... so... *coughs*

I was going to say something about looking at your watch here, but then remembered how so very yesteryear wearing a watch is. With that in mind, if you look at your watch and glance at the

Constructive

time, we seem to read it relative to another time.

Sure, it is 11:30 am, but it is really just 30 minutes until *dinner*[iv] time. Yes, it is 9:55 pm, but it is actually just 5 minutes before the 10 o'clock news. Oh blimey, it's 3:25pm and I am 25 minutes late for my meeting.

It is a curious thing. You can't touch it, you can't see it, but it has an overbearing presence.

In a wider context, we look at dates the same way. I'm writing this just before 31-December-2019. Which we view as not a singular date in the calendar, but rather the day before New Year, the end of the Decade, the day of the party, or the day of regret. You see, it is always with reference to something else.

On such a date, especially on this date as the Decade draws to a close, we often take a moment to look back and ponder.

For myself, the last Decade has been somewhat less than ideal, but don't worry I'm not going to insert a long monograph about that; it is though, through convention, a point of reflection.

As we look at where we are, and measure it

[iv]I'm going to gloss over 'dinner' vs 'lunch' here; let's just say that I am correct, and move right along.

against points in our past, we conjure up an emotional response; different for each of us.

To balance that, we also look forwards to the imagined future ahead of us.

Based on the conjured emotions of both, the historical and future views will affect how we feel right now. They are lenses of differing magnitude that focus onto our emotional selves.

So, we can see that the moment of time, and the wider perspective of date, are always read with reference to something else; past or future. It helps us function as humans. Indeed that ability to understand future consequence and assess past experiences, separate us from most of the animal kingdom.

I'm sure you can see where I am going with this? If not, then you need to work on your future prediction skills ...

"There is no time, like the present." is an expression that is both delightfully throw-away, and equally deep. Perhaps without even knowing, it manages to capture something rather special.

As we all run to a late-meeting, panic about a missed birthday, worry about our future, long for the past; we gloss over something - the present.

Constructive

As we look in both directions in our life-timeline, we forget that we have another state - *our present*.

I have written before[v], within the context of travel, about how the addiction of destinations causes us to miss the wonder of the journey itself. The same thing can be said of time. We ironically spend such a lot of *time* pondering, that we forget to enjoy the moment.

By any measure, our moment is just that; fleeting and unmeasurable. You can choose to view it in that vain, unimportant. You can chose to view it, as a secret freebie in our existence.

I have long been fascinated by the in-between, and the edges of existence. I have written[8] about my perception of reality versus actual reality; that dangerous but also colourful expression of self.

Our modernist influenced society and pressures, talk about moving forward and looking back. We are coerced into ignoring the magical gift of the moment.

The stillness of existence; the point in our journey of life that is between the destinations.

It doesn't fix anything, it doesn't change any-

---

[v] See, *Journey; semi-colon.*

thing. What it does do though, is create that third sense of self, which can often be a shelter from the frantic storm of life.

As we push into a new decade, try the present, it is the freebie of life and it is available to all.

Constructive

Trying to remember

It's all specifically sketchy.

50,555 & 1,499. That's the number of photos & videos that I have taken, not including 20 years of analogue snaps and film.

I'm not someone who takes a lot of photos, but obviously I do apparently take slightly more than some.

The reason I know those numbers, which I know look numerically lovely but which I can promise you are actual, is because of some recent archiving.

A couple of years back, I noticed that I seem to have developed a problem in remembering photos. I mean, I can recall images and photos, I just can't seem to place them into a coherent timeline.

For example, I have a fantastically clear image in my mind of the ancient woodlands near me. Absolutely no idea from *when* that was. Nope, not a dicky-bird. I don't think it was this year, but other than that... nothing. I'm not overly worried about it; the specific time something was taken is less important than the image itself.

It's like there are all these *things* in my head. Some are slowly floating along, others are racing along, but none of them seem to be linked together. Sure, I can sometimes use some deductive reasoning to work it out, but it's not always obvious.

One of the delightful side effects of this, is that I can never find anything. I have an extremely clear memory of holding it in my hand, but I have no idea whether that was last month or 20 years ago. So, I have a boat load of *stuff* that I know I own, but I have absolutely no idea *where*. Before you start to worry on my behalf, I have long since moved past the stage of worry, I'm now on the stage of shrug-laughter about it.

Anyway, let's pull this train of thought back to those numbers.

A couple of years ago, I determined that I should attempt to pull all of the digital images &

Trying to remember

videos I had taken, into some kind of archive. Part of it was driven by my lack of capacity to remember where the heck they were. Part of it was that I knew some of the *devices* they were on, were getting to the end of their life. I had also recently found a small stack of SD cards, that I assumed were empty only to discover that they had photos on. It was time to take action.

So, I purchased a 3 terabyte[vi] hard disk, and started copying them all onto that. I optimistically labelled the folder "Photos ALL", and started copying. My vague plan was to get everything in one place, then worry about what I was going to do with it all later.

It took ages to find them all, then copy. I've lost count the number of old Nokia phones I've had to charge, then start, then inspect, then workout how to get the 15 photos off of the old device[vii]. I wasn't really taking note of the numbers, just blindly copying into the folder.

The total in that particular folder currently stands at 36,824, and cover 20 years. That obviously doesn't include the 13,731 living in Apple's

---

[vi]Moderately large at the time.
[vii]This usually involved sending photo one at a time over bluetooth, using oddly structured menu systems.

photo ecosystem.[viii]

Fab. Now what?

I didn't much fancy previewing all those, one by one, so figured the best approach was to organise them into year-month groups. I didn't much fancy doing that either. So, I wrote some clever(ish) computer-thingy[ix] to do it for me. It didn't really help.[x]

OK, on a positive note, it was all being backed up now and was lovely and safe. I did have an urge, or perhaps an obligation, to take some time to actually look at them.

How do you even do that? If I took just 5 seconds to look at a photo, and I did that continuously for 3 hours a day, it would take me over 23 *days*. I didn't much fancy that either.

Why then, was I bothering? Why did I feel an overwhelming urge to keep them all safe?

I've been over-thinking this, for some time. I think it is something to do with *identity*. As we take photos of things, places, people, ourselves, it

---

[viii] Extracting photos out of the Apple ecosystem, is fiddly at best.

[ix] It was a BASH script.

[x] It actually helped a little.

creates a storybook in our minds. In some curious way, it seems to provide some kind of self-identity. Sure, it's not the only thing that does that, but it is certainly part of that internal process. If that is the case, then there is a worry that if we loose those images, then we will be loosing something of our storybook; loosing a bit of our identity.

I have *feelings* when I randomly look at photos I've taken. Sometimes positive, sometimes not; that feeling though is very real.

I can't quite put my finger on whether it's the actual image itself, or it is the memory of what I was feeling at the time. Is the image itself the magic, or is that image just the mental nudge required to recall the memory, of the feeling?

Either way, it cemented the notion that I should attempt to do something with these 50 thousand photos. Should I just print them all out? I know that sounds crazy, but at least I would have a *physical backup* of them all. So, I worked out the cost of that. Erm, no thank you!

Perhaps I should just be happy with the fact they are not lost. I should be happy, but it just doesn't cut it. I want more, I want to remember and re-experience all those times.

Constructive

Dear reader, if you were expecting some kind of magical answer, that you could also apply to your own stack of digital imagery, then you will be disappointed. I just don't think there is a simple answer to this.

What I do think though, is that perhaps I'm approaching this from the wrong angle. Perhaps I shouldn't be looking at the actual photos.

As I think back to the times of cine-film and photo-slides of yesteryear, there was a strong theatrical element to it. It was a real pantomime getting it all setup, then mucking around with the curtains, and the lighting. Then making sure that grandma with the dodgy knee could see the screen. Then making sure that everyone had a drink. Then finally looking at the images. Then talking about them, then going backwards to look at some again.

It was as much about the *process of looking at* the images, as the images themselves.

So, I've made a decision. I'm going to get myself a nice drink, make myself comfortable, turn off the internet, take off my watch, put my phone on silent, then ... Then I'm going to flick through each and every photo. It will take as long as it takes. I will just enjoy the *process* as well as the *images*.

Sometimes you just need to accept, that the journey and process, can be as important as the conclusion.

Constructive

The wrong way

Perspective is everything.

In the garden there is a big round hole. It's about 3 feet deep, and has a blue edge to it. It's full of water. It doesn't work.

Some of us have actual physical todo lists. Some of us have digital todo lists. Some of us have mental todo lists. I have none of those. I have no todo lists, quite simply because my brain doesn't work at all well with them. They cause some kind of short-circuit. I've learnt that it is just best not to have them.

In what I can only explain as a blatant outrageous act of defiance, fixing this broken circle of water, managed to create its own todo list. It was a todo list of a single item. "Fix water thing". Having created itself, it then had the audacity to lodge itself into my mind. There is sat.

Sometimes a thought would bump into it. I could feel it. Now, with that single "proper" todo list item in there, one would naturally think that it would get resolved nice and quickly.

It was.

It sat around for a couple of years, and then that singular todo item got addressed ... last Saturday.

Permit me to lay out the vastness of the task in hand. The circular water thing, was a small pond. The broken thing, was a fountain pump. I know, it's a lot to keep in your head at one time.

From about the age of 5, I can remember my father fixing things. He would not only fix things, but he would improve things. I remember our TV which had a slider for the volume control, and touch channel changer. It had 8 channels, although obviously there was only BBC1, BBC2 & ITV; 3 channels. Want to change channel or adjust the volume, then just walk over to it and do it. Simple. Dad wanted to improve that. So he built a little black box with 8 buttons & a dial. He then ran a cable into the TV, and wired it directly into the TV. We now had a remote control.

The wrong way

It seemed like magic to me.

As I got older, our car often needed repairing. It was a 1977 Triumph 2500 PI Salon. A straight-six engine, with mechanical fuel injection. It was fabulous. It had a mind of its own. It needed maintenance.

I remember something being wrong with the gearbox. It had 4 forward gears, with overdrive on 3rd & 4th; it was complicated. So, armed with a Haynes Manual,[9] Dad took to fixing it. Taking the gearbox out, using an old Castrol GTX oil-can to soften the fall as it dropped onto the garage floor; it was a bit of a mission. Next came a total disassembly. Spring, cogs, rods, all sorts - spread all over the garage.

I don't recall what the actual problem was, but I remember the gearbox was taken out 5 times, over the next 10 days. In the end, it was fixed. Dad fixed it.

With all that history behind me, it was my turn.

Step one, check that it is broken. Throw the switch. Nothing. OK, a positive start. Step two involved removing an unnecessarily large amount of rockery and garden statues. Step three was more free-form.

Constructive

OK, don't worry I'm not going to spend the next 1000 words giving a blow-by-blow account of every single step; just stick with me for a moment.

Checking that the 240 volt cable, that was "protected" with some tape, was good (ignore the rust). I had to confront the fact that it could be a broken pump.

This hadn't worked for at least 2 years, so the water was... well lets just say *green*.

I fished out the pump. As a sanity check, I flicked the power switch to it. It coughed and then worked. Excellent, I wouldn't have to undo all that nasty tape around that nasty connector-block-hack thing.

I lowered the coughing pump just below the waterline. It worked. So, what was the problem? I looked at the water. It had settled, and was clear. OK, so perhaps it just needed a kick. Great, that was an easy fix.

So I installed it back into the same position. Flicked the power switch... cough, then nothing.

Pulled the pump out; it worked. Put it just below the surface; it worked. Looked at the water; it was clear.

So we had a working pump, "working" water,

The wrong way

but combined they didn't work.

I'm sure you have had the same kind of feeling. You know, when two things work separately, but combined they just don't at all work. Sometimes it is in your place of work. Sometimes it is in the relationship between your loved ones. Sometimes it is between your kids. Put them together, and they just don't work right.

I finally did work out what the problem was. There was nothing wrong with the pump, there was nothing wrong with the water. The problem was that the pump had to pull in the water, to pump it up. That inlet was pointing downwards. It wasn't pulling in the water, it was pulling in the sludge at the bottom.

I didn't need to change the water. I didn't need to fix the pump. All I had to do was to re-orient it, so it pulled the water from above.

Sometimes the reason that things don't work, is not because of the individuals. It is not the combination of those individuals. It is just that we are looking at it from the wrong view point.

Sometimes you just need to look at the broken thing, from a different position, to see that it really isn't broken at all. It just needs a small adjustment of perspective.

The pump wasn't broken. The water wasn't broken. One just needed a small change of position; fixed.

Stressful Calm

It's not the thing, it's the control of the thing.

For my 30th Birthday, I went on a rallying course. I got to drive a range of cars, including a Ford Sierra Cosworth with a racing gearbox. For my 40th Birthday, I got to drive an Aston Martin DBS with a manual gearbox, and a Ferrari F430 with a flappy-paddle gearbox. Both around the Silverstone race track.

Let's scroll forward to the present time; I'm almost 48[xi]. A few weeks ago, I got to drive a Mercedes-AMG GT3. The other week, I got to drive a Ferrari 488 GT3.

As I recall, the handling of the Sierra was predictable, nice and easy. It was the racing gearbox

---

[xi] Older by the time you read this.

Constructive

---

that was harsh. I can remember changing down from 3rd to 2nd, being a little too harsh with the clutch, and was rewarded with a rear wheel lock up. Swiftly followed by some expletives from the instructor next to me.

I have clearer memories of my time at Silverstone. The Ferrari was a breeze to drive. Although fast, the flappy-paddle (steering wheel mounted) gearbox was a delight. No need of a clutch, just flick the right paddle to go up a gear, and the left one to go down a gear. The simplicity of that, allowed much more concentration of the craft of not-crashing it.

The Aston Martin was a different story. By the time I got to drive it, the track was a little wet. That coupled with the manual gear box, made it an extra challenge. The connection with the road was fantastic, but changing gear whilst sliding around a corner that you had approached a little too fast, was *interesting* to say the least. I can say that at points I was borderline scared of crashing this expensive piece of kit. It was though, the most rewarding to drive.

Now, I'm sure you didn't sign up for a motoring narrative, but there is an actual point to all this; isn't there always?

Stressful Calm

In recent times, driving the AMG and the Ferrari, the jump into GT3 cars is a big one. They are raw and somewhat unforgiving. The AMG with its large 6.3L V12 engine, is rammed full of low-down torque, and has a quiet confidence to it as well as a great soundtrack! On the other hand, the Ferrari with its turbo enhanced V8 is more of a handful. I drive it with an aggressive setup, which makes for fast lap times but it can be a little *twitchy* in the corners.

In the time between racing the AMG and the Ferrari, I also designed a Tokyo inspired 4 floor house. It has cute little small rooms, stacked in an offset pattern. The exterior is clad with turquoise tiles, and the top floor, housing the master bedroom, has a glass roof to allow you to enjoy the stars.

Maybe I've given the game away there... Some clarity is perhaps overdue.

The rallying and Silverstone, took place in real life. The rest didn't.

The GT3 cars are part of an incredibly realistic racing simulation. With laser-scanned tracks and detailed car and tyre physics, it is pretty close to the real thing; it's an e-sport. With live coverage of races, and real-life racing drivers competing, it really is something.

The building design work, was in *The Sims 4*. My effort did receive positive reviews, and has been downloaded a number of times.

OK, so what am I getting at here? I'm glad you asked.

The e-sports sim-racing is super stressful. There is nothing quite like racing around Monza at 180mph, against 20 other people in real time, trying to concentrate on not missing your braking point at that first corner, whist not slamming into the Lamborghini Huracan GT3 Evo beside you who is trying a doomed-to-failure overtaking manoeuvre!

The Sim 4 house build, is super calming. With the light music, spending ages pondering whether a light oak floor would better match the wallpaper, than a white-washed birch floor.[xii]

During these times of isolation[xiii], some tell us not to get stressed about it all. To take up learning a new language, or to think about trying out yoga. There is an undercurrent of not-to-panic advice, and not panicking is fantastic advice.

[xii] I chose the birch.

[xiii] This was written during the COVID-19 lockdowns of 2020-2021.

As a person who has rapidly cycling Bipolar, I am acutely aware of my current (changing) mental health; I obviously monitor it closely. Coupled with my medication, I have tried all sorts of approaches to remove stress from my life. In essence, I have been forced to take a stress-free view of life.

I have though, discovered a curious thing. I have found that it is not about removing stress. It is about controlling it, or the lack of having control of it.

E-sport racing is super-stressful. Designing Sims 4 builds isn't at all stressful. I have found that I feel a little more balanced partaking in both sides of the stress-coin. Just forcing one or the other, feels... well it feels forced. It feels a little artificial.

It is not about stress vs calm, it is about the *choice* of stress or calm. If I feel like racing, then I will. If I feel like building, then I will. If I don't feel like either, then that's fine too.

We don't all have control of our circumstances or the amount and kind of stress in our lives. The current isolation will have no doubt intensified those views, and perhaps created new stress-challenges.

Constructive

The key message of, not panicking, of being more considerate of others, of damn well staying at home when instructed to do so. It is all really about taking control of yourself. It isn't about removing stress at all, no matter what celebrities tell us.

Turns out that the stress that is bad, is the stress that we have no control over.

The Words of Movies

Self-regulated joy.

The other day, I watched a truly terrible movie. It wasn't that it had a poor budget, it wasn't that it had an unskilled cast, but it was still one of the most rubbish movies that I've seen in ages. I am, of course, talking about the $300 million *Justice League*.

Now, I'm aware of the production problems that caused a certain amount of *complexity*, but that just doesn't explain it all. If I'm honest, the total lack of merit to the movie has been bothering me a little.

I've seen one heck of a lot of movies in my time, from no-budget in obscure genres, to the kind you would expect. Some I certainly couldn't watch again, and some were also just as rubbish.

Constructive

So, what am I wittering on about then?

Well, given the resources at hand, I guess I was just a little shocked at the end result. I should say that I'm not a DC Comics kind of guy, although I will admit to queueing up to see the first Batman film, with Michael Keaton.[10]

For me, it all comes down to story-telling and how effective you are at doing that. I may not agree with the story, I may not like the story, the story may be very abstract, I may not like the method of telling the story ... but there should still be a story.

When a movie-maker is telling a story, they do have a tricky task. One of pacing. The movie is 2 hours and 9 minutes long. It is the same length for everyone who watches it. They have the almost impossible task trying to make it understandable for everyone, at a pace and speed that everyone can cope with and likes. Having a story that the audience wants to hear, you also need to tell it at a pace that they want to consume. Mix into that the requirements of the Studio, and all the other people who have their fingers in the pie, and it really is a wonder that they ever work!

In writing a book, I am using words to create a scene or to evoke an emotion; to tell a story. In once sense this is much like a movie-maker. They have to do the same thing, except for them the *consumer* gets to visually witness the scene. The latter is much easier to consume. You can see this in a very obvious way; people talk and chatter when watching a movie, people don't do the same when reading a book. The movie requires less brain power to enjoy, than the book.

I'm not saying that one is better than the other, I am just saying that they have a different set of problems to solve when telling the story.

There is one big difference, that for me makes the book a much richer experience. The book is a *different length for each person.*

Everyone is different, thank goodness, and our desired speed at consuming story-based entertainment is also different. The movie has a fixed speed at which it runs, and that is the same for each of those different people. The book can be read at your own speed; at your own leisure.

I'm not a fast reader at all, which is kind of strange, since I consider myself a fast writer. I don't know why this is, and it used to bother me a lot. Then I realised that it isn't a race. When you return a book back to the library, they don't ask how long it took you to read it, then add your

Constructive

timing to some giant universal ledger, which is then published in all the newspapers on a monthly basis. Nope, no one cares.

There is a book that I've read loads of times, it is called Eon by Greg Bear.[11] It's Science Fiction, and there is something about that book that I just like. When I read it for the first time, there were parts of it that I just didn't understand. There were some technical aspects that were explained a little too fast. There were some character names that I just couldn't quite pronounce correctly in my head. In all of those cases, I just read the passage again. Similarly if there was a paragraph that I thought was particularly good, then I would re-read it again.

You just can't do that with a movie, especially if you are watching it with others.

My point? With Movies, the pace is enforced. With Books the pace is personal.

In a wider sense, there are a lot of things in our lives where the pace is enforced onto us. The things where we can self-pace seem to be few and far between. The truth of it is, that some of the enforced pace is just down to convention and peer-pressure. There may not be any actual real *reason* for that particular pace.

We all aspire to have a better life-balance; it's not a straightforward task to find it. Perhaps though, taking a look at those enforced paced activities might help.

There is an enforced pressure in watching a movie, there is a self-regulated joy in reading a book. I'm happier being more like a book, and less like a movie.

Constructive

Connections

Joining the dots from A to unknown.

If you are anything like me, then you will spend a lot of time on YouTube just randomly clicking on stuff. It really is an astounding piece of social engineering. You can amble on there, with the intent of watching (again) that rather wonderful Abba video. At the end of the video it will suggest something else; down the right side of the page, it will also suggest other thing that you might be interested in. So the journey begins.

When I was a kid, going to school on a bus, we would often play the Word-Association game. It was simple enough, and can work with 2 or many players. Someone gets to start, and chooses a word. The next person has to choose another word, but it must be related to the previous word.

Constructive

The relationship can be as tenuous as you want, but when challenged you should be able to explain it. For example; Wine -\> Grapes -\> Ghostbusters. With the last jumping being explained as, "people think of grapes as green, when people think of the Ghostbusters movie, they remember the cute ghost-monster who is also green." You get the idea. The entertainment value in the game, is to stop at some point and wonder at how far away the first word is from the last.

Back to YouTube. It is doing the same kind of thing. It somehow takes you down a route of tenuous links, into a rabbit hole of entertainment and wonder.

Whilst on such a journey I stumbled upon, which sounds like I actually had a choice, perhaps more accurately *coerced*, a wonder.

His name is Marc Verdiell, you can find out more about him at Curious Marc.[12]

He had previously restored a 1930s Teletype machine, specifically the Model 15 Teletype. These machines were used to send text a few miles away to another machine, which would then automatically print it out onto paper, like a typewriter would do; just text. Having read the typed page, the operator could type back a response. The whole machine is mechanical.

He wondered if he could connect up this 1930s bit of mechanical kit, to a modern computer & get it to perform 2-way communication. As you may expect, there were quite a number of *challenges* in doing that. He did of course succeed. It's remarkable to watch.

Anyway it got me thinking, which granted doesn't take much effort, about connections. He demonstrated that you can connect something from one era to another era.

Much of our social connections are within the same social bubble. You can *reason* why you have a connection to someone or something. This might be because of geography, or it might just be down to feeling safe with things that we know. When we seek out, or stumble upon, new potential connections, there is that internal sanity-check that measures it against those previous connections. It is self-regulating. Sure, some of us are better at this than others, but it still does happen at some level.

In the above example, Marc takes two items that have no default right to have a connection, and connects them. There is the extensive and impressive technical skill in doing that, but there is also something else going on here.

Marc demonstrated the ability to think in the abstract, to consider the inconsiderable. He then chose to act on that.

I find myself, that there is some value in doing that. I mean, considering the inconsiderable. Not to follow through and act on it, but to do the *thought* bit before the action.

In doing so, you are coercing your mind to take an unfamiliar route. You are asking it to go on an associative walk into the wilderness. Going from the initial thought to the next, to the next, to the next. Seeing if there is a route to the final objective.

Would it be possible to walk across an entire country in a straight line? Could you record the Internet as noise onto a wax cylinder? Can you really mix fire and play-dough? Could I knock on my neighbour's door, and have a friendly conversation without being creepy about it?

I'm not saying that you should *do* any of those things, but in thinking about the possibilities you are entering into a *philosophical gym*.

Just as we should endeavour to exercise our physical self, I think there is merit in trying to exercise our mental self too.

Constructive

Episode v Season

Perspective is more than you think.

On the 24th March 2020, Disney launched Disney+[13] here in the UK. It presented an opportunity for me. You see, I'd not seem all of the Marvel movies, or MCU[xiv] as they are often referred. Sure, I had seen most, but there was a slab that I just hadn't watched.

Anyway, given this opportunity to watch them, I set about working out the best order. Obviously others had done the same, and it turns out that the current recommended method, is to watch them in *timeline order*.[14] That is to say, not in the order that they're made and released, but rather the chronological order in which they are set in. So

---

[xiv] Marvel Cinematic Universe.

for example, the second movie would be *Captain Marvel*,[15] released in 2019 but set in 1995.

Last night that particular viewing project came to its conclusion, with *Avengers: Endgame*.[16]

It was an interesting experience watching all the movies in close succession. I mean I didn't binge watch, but you get the idea. Whilst each movie had its own merits, the overarching story arc was impressive and satisfying.

I have fond memories of watching *Star Trek: The Next Generation*,[17] followed of course by *Star Trek: Voyager*.[18] Around the same time, I was also watching *Babylon 5*.[19] Once again, they all had their own merits, but their approach to story telling was quite different.

Star Trek's primary focus seemed to be to make sure that each episode could be viewed & enjoyed in isolation. Sure, there were threads of ongoing story lines, but they were few and far between. You could be certain, that in the last few minutes of the episode, everything would be nicely resolved. Not in every single case, but in most. It has to be said, that this approach worked to its advantage, as new viewers could just arrive half way into a random series and still enjoy it immensely.

Babylon 5 was an entirely different matter. Best described as a *space opera*, it was vast in scale and ambition. Entirely written by one man, J. Michael Straczynski, from 1993 to 1998 spanning over 5 seasons and 111 episodes, followed up by 4 movies to conclude the story arcs. It is said that whilst writing season 1 he knew what season 5 would be. With complex storylines that span multiple episodes and multiple seasons, it really does show. You can't just dip in and out of it, you'd loose 70% of what is going on. At the end of each episode, the story is very rarely wrapped up. Still considered by many as the greatest sci-fi show of all time.

All this obviously got me thinking; you won't be at all surprised.

Star Trek is a collection of chicken nuggets. Babylon 5 is a 9 course meal. MCU is a Sunday Roast dinner. They are all in the *speculative fiction* genre, but have different things to offer. Which is fine by the way, and does not mean one is better than the other.

The other day, I was in the garden shuffling around. I spotted a particularly interesting stone. I picked it up, and just spent a few moments looking at it; pushing it around in my hand. Then

Constructive

placed it back. It was a tiny moment, focused and rich.

"It's all about perspective" - you often hear that phrase. It's banded about like a packet of biscuits at a knitting club.

I think that perspective isn't just about the angle of view, field of vision, or scope. In that throwaway phrase, it is trying to get you to stop looking at whatever it is you are looking at, take a step back, and take in another view. To look at what is going on around you.

You can imagine that quite easily; me placing the stone back on the ground, standing up, and looking at the whole garden.

The reverse is also true, take a moment to take a closer look at the detail, rather than just viewing the big picture.

It's all about where to look, and when.

Which, I think is entirely missing the point. It actually isn't about looking at all. It is surely something much more than that.

When I was chatting about MCU, Star Trek, Babylon 5, I was describing what my expectations were of each of them. How they measured up against that expectation. However, that exception was already set. The very fact that there existed a *timeline viewing order* for MCU, suggested a certain viewing expectation. Sure, I could change my *perception* from looking at each movie on its own, or as a group, but it was always within that pre-set expectation.

I believe that the real meaning of the phrase *put things into perspective*, is not just that we should change our viewing angle, of the visual interpretation of the what is before us. I believe that it is also suggesting that we should reset our mental view of it too.

That change of perspective, also has a change of mindset about it too. Further, I believe that it isn't just saying that we should *change it* but rather that we should *delete the previous one*, then *reset* into something *fresh and new*.

Sometimes you just need to go from looking at a single pebble, to a garden view; from one to another.

Sometimes you need to look at the whole garden, and realise that it also contains pebbles.

Constructive

Einstein's Weather

It's all about boats and twigs.

I'm not sure what the weather is like where you are, or I guess *when* you are. It's been sunshiny here. Not the kind of basking sunshine, but it seems like a taste of the start of summer.

The next day, it was still sunny. Nice blue skies. It was lovely.

Then, it was sunny with a blustery wind. Not the kind to knock you off your feet, or to blow anything substantial over. No, it was just *blowy*.

Having been tending towards the warmer end of things, I've had my bedroom window on the first latch. As I lay there, trying as always to trick myself into sleeping, the wind was really whistling through the gap. It was swirling around. As it hit each edge, a different tone filled the room; whistle to drone.

Which got me thinking. Obviously, about water, sticks, and of course, stones. Not in that order.

Weather has the strange capacity to provoke thought. In the sunshine we can feel euphoric and optimistic. In the rain we can feel either refreshed, or depressingly soaked. A storm outside, can make us feel cosy and safe inside.

I think that is why, when asked, I have said that I would never want to live in a place where the weather was uniform. I need that change.

Change is a difficult thing though. When it is forced upon us, it can be distressing. When it is instigated by us, it can fulfilling. When it doesn't happen, it can either be comforting or frustrating.

Someone once said to me that, *it is easier to steer a moving boat.* They were speaking both practically, and metaphorically.

When I started on this writing experiment, it was for a whole stack of reasons. The main reason, was that I wanted to keep the boat moving. Well actually, I wanted to start the boat moving.

That notion has become more nuanced in recent times, and I now think of it with reference to a flowing river.

Some choose to sit and watch the river rush by. Some need or want, to stand in the middle of the river. They are like a reed that is holding steadfast, as the water rushes around them. As the water races by, the effort needed to hold on and the speed of the water, creates the *rush* feeling of movement. For some in the river, they are pebbles, pulled down onto the riverbed. Trying to make themselves as smooth as possible to let the water flow over them, with as little fuss as possible.

I'm sure we have all experienced those kind of emotive experiences.

Before I started this, I was the pebble. After starting this, I was the reed.

Recently, I have seen another alternative. One where everything can rush by, but which is also still. The twig in the river is both stationary in the water, but also moving along. Letting the river dictate the journey. So, for a little while, I'm going to give that a try; the twig.

Albert Einstein's theory of General Theory of Relativity,[20] although referring to *Time*, says that in principle you could measure things by their relation or relativity to yourself.

Constructive

To those sitting on the riverside, to the reed, even to the pebble, the twig is racing along. The twig's view of it is different, it can see the riverbank, the pebble, the reed, moving past. From their own relative perspective though, they are still & calm. They are also travelling *somewhere*.

In identifying as the twig, it is just an expression of the riverbank moving by; the river is the journey, that will undoubtedly lead to *somewhere*.

The most important thing though, is that my metaphorical boat will still be moving along.

Effort v Effort

It's all about amount and location.

It was the other day, that I decided to go for a drive. Not a drive to a specific location, or a drive for a specific reason. I just wanted to go for a *drive*.

I guess it must be a family thing, as my father would often enjoy the actual *drive* bit of going somewhere.

So with the current restrictions[xv] of movement, I hadn't actually been out in the car for ... Well, if I think about it, I'm not quite sure how long; maybe a month or so.

The first challenge was locating my car keys. I've said on many occasions, that I have specific

---

[xv] COVID-19 driven restrictions of 2020-21.

Constructive

locations for certain things; keys, wallet, glasses, phone, medication. Some think I've overstated the importance of that. Well, today it paid off. My keys were in the *official* place. (I've noted this for future discussions on the matter).

Flushed with success, and remembering to take my wallet for that *if something happens you should have some bendy money* situation. I exited the house and walked towards my car. For those of you who have been paying attention, it's a 2008 Mercedes E220 currently with 175,000 miles on the clock. It has been a long time, and it was with the familiar greeting, I opened the door and got in. It was its usual delightfully comfortable self.

Keys in the ignition, random set of lights appear, turn ... engine half turns over, and then nothing. Oh, guess the battery is dead. Perhaps I should have started it every couple of weeks or so.

Still, I was determined to go for that drive to nowhere.

It was then I remembered that I had a telescope. It's not a massive telescope, but it is of a reasonable size. You can use it for planet watching, as well as deep sky stuff. It has a set of electronic wizardry, which means that it knows where all the *stuff* in the sky is. Once stable on its substantial tripod, you just plug in the date & time, located 3 random bright things in the sky. It can then work out exactly where it is on the planet & present you with a database of things to look at or position on. It's actually quite clever.

I remember setting it up for the first time, in the front room. Lots of bits and bobs, and cables, and remote controls, and glass eyepieces, and a heavy tripod. But it seemed straightforward enough. So, later that night I took all the parts outside, found a nice dark spot. Turns out that it is *slightly* more of a challenge assembling it all in the pitch black.

After some considerable effort, and a few bad words, it was up and running. It had its own power source, and we were *cooking with gas*, so to speak.

You can spend a heck of a lot of money on astronomy, and some of it is just expensive because it is tagged as astronomy. You know, like a computer mouse that is £15, but when they stick the *gamer* tag on it paint it black, they charge you £35.

My 'scope needed a reliable power source. It could run on 8 small AA batteries, but in chilly winter temperatures, they tend to drain and be unreliable. The solution is to buy a special *astronomy* battery pack. It has branding on it, and costs around £120. That seemed a bit much. So, I decided to ignore that approach, and get something else.

Back to the car that doesn't start. I bet you thought I'd forgotten that.

The astronomy battery shortcut, was a car-quick-start device. A small/medium sized battery, with a light, a standard *cigarette connection*, and even 2 USB charging ports. The standard connection of course connected to my 'scope. It also had 2 jump-start red & black grips.

It was in the garage, and ready to rock-n-roll, so to speak.

Now, the battery on a Mercedes, is located in the boot/trunk. I think the rationale, is that if you are in a head-on crash, then by having the battery at the back, there is a better chance that all the electronics will still work. The weight distribution is also better, and it of course gives them more space up front to put other stuff.

So, all the stuff came out of the boot. It's quite a large battery I have to say, and I was a little worried that the Jump-start wasn't up to the challenge. I know that *large* is a relative term. To give you an idea, using a current unit of measurement that you will be familiar with, it's around 408 boxes of matches size.

Jump-start connected up, turn key. Started first time.

Disconnect, put it back into the garage, connect it up to charge. We are off on our random drive. OK, it took a while, but we are off.

The drive was lovely, and I didn't really go anywhere specific, just a nice 65 mile drive through some countryside.

After several weeks, the poor little jump-start battery, was still charging. It obviously took one heck of a lot of effort for it to get the car going; it's still not fully charged.

Last Thursday, when I'm due to write this piece. I was thinking that I really should think about what to write. So I took a few minutes, in fact it was probably less than a minute, and I immediately came up with this idea. It was easy.

I had the idea, of what I wanted to say. I didn't though, know how I was going to get there. I had no idea at all how I was going to get to the endpoint, the conclusion. No matter, don't panic. It will arrive in my mind soon. Well I can tell you, that it took several days of effort to work that one out. In fact, I'm writing this on Saturday.

Starting was a breeze, but finishing it in a way that I was happy with, was a massive effort.

Which thankfully gets me to my point.

Going on the random drive, took one heck of a lot of *effort to start*. Once started, it was super *easy to finish*. Writing this piece was super *easy to start*, but was really *difficult to finish*.

They both required the same amount of effort. One required it all at the *start*, the other required it all at the *end*.

We often see effort in different ways. Often though, it is just the same amount, expressed and positioned at a different time.

Putting a little *effort*, into treating *effort* in the same way, means that the overall amount of *effort* required, seems to smooth out and somehow seem like less *effort*.

The Longhand World

Old maps and pencils, will improve your world.

As I mentioned the other day[xvi], I went for a drive. It wasn't to a particular place, or for a particular reason. It was just a drive.

During said drive, I decided to switch on the map in the car. Again, I wasn't planning on using the route/navigation part of it; I just wanted to see the world scroll by on it. I'd previously configured it up so that North is always up. Which means that the map doesn't rotate as you drive; drive south and you are going downwards on the screen. You know, like all bendy paper maps work.

The car has maps of the entirety of Europe; every single road. You can ask it to plot a course to

---

[xvi] See, *Effort v Effort*.

Constructive

Zurich, and it will do just that. Lovely. However, given the age of the car and of the maps, I prefer to think of them as more of an artistic impression than a technical drawing.

I'm a great fan of maps, I just love maps. I love the notion that someone has actually visited each and every place on the map, and drawn it on a map. I know that's not true these days, with satellites and related technical wizardry in place, but in yesteryear it felt somehow more tactile.

In 1747, King Louis XV of France commissioned cartographer Cesar-Francois Cassini de Thury, to draw as exact a map of France as possible.[21] Cassini was an experience cartographer, and boldly stated that it would take 20 years to produce. Not having access to satellite telemetry in 1747, Cassini used the *geodesic triangulation* technique to get the raw data. This essentially meant taking 6 foot long chains, laying them on the ground in a specific fashion, and documenting the measurements. It was to be produced on the scale of *one line* (one twelfth of an inch) on the map to 100 *toises* on the ground, that is 1/86,400. A *toises* was a standard unit of measurement used in France until 1812; 6 feet long. Interestingly the precise exact measure of a *toises*, since before 1394 was taken from an iron bar embedded in the wall

The Longhand World

of the Grand Chatelet.[22]

Anyway, in fulfilling the cartography commission, Cassini had to visit each and every part of France. In the end it took 50 years to complete, spanned 2 Cassini generations, with the final map requiring 182 sheets.[23]

By its very nature, it was the longhand method of creating a map. Yes, I know it was the only method, at the time.

I remember as a child, a man knocking on the door of our house, newly built in 1984. He was from the Ordnance Survey, and wanted to take a look at the external shape of the house. Why? Well he wanted to draw it onto the new Ordnance Survey map of this area. How cool is that?

Well, that got me thinking. About writing.

My current tool of choice for writing, is my 2016 12 inch MacBook[xvii]. It weighs a mere 920 grams, at its thinnest point is just 3.5mm thick, has a 10 hour battery, and having no cooling fans is completely silent. I've written a lot of words using this delightful piece of kit.

As I've previously eluded to, well actually I've specifically stated, I use a piece of software called

---

[xvii]this has since changed, but we will gloss over that.

Ulysses[xviii]. Again, it's super lightweight, and doesn't get in your way.

I'm using that setup right now[xix].

In thinking about the long hand nature of early cartography, pre-satellite. I got to thinking about *writing* pre-computer, or even pre-typewriter. Don't worry, I will spare you (this time) a diversion into the history of the typewriter.

Writing a lengthy prose, using nothing but a pen or pencil and some paper, is almost unheard of these days.

We are all so trained in reading typeset works, I wonder if we are even generally capable of reading a 10 page hand written document. The end result of Cassini's endeavours was not a book of measurements, but a map. The end result of this, is an electronic document nicely formatted containing these words for you to easily read.

It's not about the end result, it is about the process.

The author James Patterson, prefers to write

[xviii] this has also changed, I now use Emacs in org-mode; we'll gloss over that too.

[xix] well, I was at the time of writing (see other footnotes!)

all of his novels out in longhand. Using yellow paper, and a pen.

Has the modern ease in which we can *create content* removed some of the *creative muse* of it? Well, it certainly has allowed new types of content to be created, stuff that just wouldn't be possible without that modern ease element.

But what for writing? Where we end up, is that I do wonder if my writing would be *creatively better* if I was to write it longhand. My preference would be a pencil and paper. I'm certain that it wouldn't be *technically better*, but those *fixes* can be inserted when I transcribed the handwritten art, into the precise electronic edition.

Given some extra time, perhaps next week I will just have to give that a try.

In musing about maps, I think I have concluded that in some cases, a longhand view of the World can be a richer and more fulfilling experience that the electronic shortcut variation.

Constructive

Creative Thinking

It's not always about doing *something*. It can just be about being creative in your thinking, and seeing what happens.

I believe that we are all *creative creatures*. The amount of creativity on offer, the ability need or even wish, to express and show it, is of course variable.

These chapters offer no promised outcome, they are just the consequence of some creative thinking on my part.

Creative

Creative Place

You need to find your creative place.

Here I am, sitting in a nice English country pub, writing this article. There are aged brown oak beams, propping up a bar with an appropriate selection of ale. To my left is an open fire, bathing the surroundings in a warm glow. An occasional person will toss some wood onto it, forcing an orange-yellow burst of light. There are just enough people here, to be entertainingly interesting but not too noisy. I'm sitting in a comfy leather chair, with a pint of ale in front of me, which is adding to the sense of calm that I have about me.

This is not my creative place.

Don't get me wrong, it is a delightfully pleasant and inviting place, but it isn't the geographical muse that encourages my creative thoughts.

We all have places that we like to visit. Sometimes because of the people that inhabit them; sometimes because they are beautiful. Often those places emote memories, that are themselves warm and lovely.

It's healthy to have a catalogue of such places in mind, to be called upon as needed. We often do this with music, happy music, calming music, party music, melancholic music. Why not do it with places too?

Understanding what a place has to offer, is important. Be it a feeling of safety or just somewhere to shelter from the rain. The inverse is true too. Places can often have a negative effect, for exactly the same reasons. In both cases, I think it is mentally healthy to know the lay of the land before you stumble into it.

I have to be honest, this isn't anything to do with anything that I am writing about here.

There is a cliche that a Creative Place needs to be some kind of idylic location. It needs to be like a Muse dressed in white, playing a flute.

Before we get onto what my creative place is, lets have a quiet fireside chat about the impor-

Creative Place

tance of having a creative place.

You may be someone who doesn't have much creative output; thinking that this does not apply to you. You would, be entirely wrong. Everyone is creative. What varies massively his how they express it, or even if they ever express it at all.

There are moments throughout your day, where your mind will wander. It will day-dream into an alternative state. It may be a lovely place, it may fall into a darker place with a sense of dread. This is the creative part of your brain doing its thing. Often such meandering feel random and without a sense of organisation. It can feel like you are a passenger on some kind of mind-bus. That randomness feels unsettling and can often be a cause of stress; never a good idea.

Having a creative place, can help your mind bring some organisational structure to those thoughts. That structure can in turn instil an inward sense of calm. Now don't get me wrong, I am not suggesting that all is well, that your problems are solved. No, I am suggesting that you will have more of a chance of constructively thinking about the matters in hand.

That organisation, allows you to gently get off the mind-bus and survey the situation presented before you. It may allow you to prepare for an unpleasant time, or better craft a positive experience; it's important.

In this current world which has a fascination of *things*, we are often driven to *destinations* and *places*. The things that we want to own, the places that we want to go. When considering a *creative place*, it is reasonable to view it through that particular lens. Finding your place becomes an itinerary of possibilities, and a mild feeling of panic tends as part of that search.

I started this by describing the location where I am writing this, but also expressing that this is not indeed, my creative place. Sure, it is the place that I am writing at the moment, but it is not where the creative seed for this article was sown.

That place is somewhere full of magical intent. It is a gloriously complicated landscape populated with, regret, joy, fear, and hope.

For me, it is that moment at 3:30am when I finally fall asleep. Specifically, it is that fiery space just before I fall into the abyss of the sleep landscape. That complex place in my mind that is rammed full of the intoxicating mix of fear and hope.

My *creative place*, is located squarely in my

Creative Place

mind and not an idylic physical location full of white muses playing flutes.

To be honest, it has taken many years to get this point; to arrive at this juncture.

I have to say dear reader, that having recognised the importance of a *creative place*, and in turn letting go of that responsibility of discovering a physical location, I have removed that particular stress-point and found something else.

The location in my mind, in my self, is richer and more textured than anything I could have discovered elsewhere.

Better than that, our minds are freely accessible by ourselves. Even if full of challenging content, they are in essence, the core of our creative thought and by extension our creative output.

So, as we have moved into another week, another month, another year, indeed another decade, give yourself the gift of the stillness of thought and allow those thoughts to meander into the landscape of your glorious mind.

Creative

Cracks in Reality

All the stuff in-between.

The other day I was taking a slow amble, across the Fens.[24] It was a tiny road, bordering on a track, bordering on a bridleway. Anyway, I remembered driving down this very road some 30 years before; it was equally as narrow then, but there were two things I noticed now.

(1) The road surface was certainly rougher. It was sunken on one side, which being as I was in the Fenland wasn't entirely surprising, and had its fair share of potholes.

(2) It had grass growing in the middle of the road.

Now, as I remembered driving down this road, at some speed it has to be said, I didn't remember the green smudge down the centre of the road. I do remember the green smudge of the hedges each side of the road, as I whizzed by them.

It obviously got me thinking, which I'm sure you guessed it would. In true overthinking fashion, I checked a map from 1700, of the Fenland in question. Which by the way, you can get from the wonderful *Old Maps Online* website.[25] It showed a track that follows the same route of the road, which is kind of cool. Anyway, whilst I'm sure it was then more of a track than a road, I do expect it was well-worn.

Back in the late 80s/early 90s, it had obviously got upgraded to a winding strip of tarmac, but it still had an appropriate amount of traffic. The grass before me, suggested that had changed.

Now, I'm certainly not an expert on how long it takes to grow grass in the middle of a road, but I'm guessing it is slightly longer than a rain shower and a couple of weeks.

As I continued to car-amble, I wondered what had changed, which then got derailed by a new thought; how much better the road looked.

Previously, it was just a small road. Now it was a road with some wildlife embedded into it; much more interesting. As I drove around the bend, I

Cracks in Reality

found myself being *careful* about not driving over the grass in the middle.

Time had moved the tarmac blandness, into an organically rich environment. It was delightful.

It got me thinking, again. What other stuff in our lives have space between them.

Back at home, and as I was over-pondering this very thought, I glanced out at the patio outside. Again, there was a glorious array of green stuff growing between each slab. Our instinct is to clear that all away, to jet wash the patio clean. Sure, that would look *newer*, but would it be *better*?

There is a moment, just before you fall asleep, that is calm and warm and, dare I say, fluffy. Just as you pass from the conscious into the land-of-nod. You also get the wonderful feeling as you wake up, when there isn't an alarm clock shouting at you, of being in an almost-dream-state.

Both of those have a certain mystic to them. They feel a little other-worldly. Well to me they do.

My point? Well my point is that I often spend far too much time thinking and worrying, about *stuff*. There is a need to identify the stuff, to polish the stuff, to think and decided about the stuff, to do something positive and pro-active about the stuff.

I'm starting to think, that I should be spending more time thinking and enjoying those magical things *between the stuff.*

I have no idea what I'm doing

I really don't.

So here's the thing. You lovely readers probably think that I have some comprehensive topic list of what I am going to write about. That I have some schedule to which I write. That I am disciplined in my approach to writing. That I have some formal training, in writing.

I do not; I have none of those.

Perhaps you can tell, but I've no special training in writing, and to be honest, I'm not very good a keeping to a schedule either. As for the topic list, well let's just say that it's more of a random thought-cloud than a list.

Creative

The training part, or rather the lack of it, is worth chatting about for a moment. You see, I believe that we all have words in us. I mean, we all manage to talk and to engage in a conversation; some better than others. But, we all have that basic skill. I see my kind of writing, as just a small extension of me chatting. I'm just chatting to this screen, rather than to a person. I think that matters, because a lot of people are afraid of writing because they think they need to have some special skill or training. Sure, there are some things that you need to learn and tune, but those skills are irrelevant if you don't have any words in the first place! Get some words down, and you can then muck around with structure, pace and possibly grammar.

Having a time that you write, just like having a time that you may exercise, or a time that you watch the telly-box, can be helpful. It can act as a nudge to get you going. I find that the nudge is only necessary if I am doing something that I don't enjoy. The more I enjoy something, the less of a nudge I need to do it. That stands to reason, surely. But wait a moment, I have to publish something[26] every single week; Tuesday at noon, in case you didn't spot that. How does that work? Surely you need a schedule to make that happen,

I have no idea what I'm doing

I hear none of you saying.

I just need to make sure that I have *something* to publish. As mentioned previously[xx], my capacity for writing is mixed. So I tend to write when I am able. That might be at lunchtime on a Saturday, or it might be at 3am on a Wednesday. As long as something is written, then that is just fine and dandy. I have found that giving myself some flexibility in when I write, rather than sticking to a super-strict schedule, has removed some of the stress and pressure; which is a good thing for me. Interestingly, at least for me, I have found that my writing has become more fluid and less formal in nature as a result; I like that.

Now, let's meander onto the topic of topics. This is a bit of a tricky one.

I once saw a YouTube video, from someone who I respect, talking about how you create an effective YouTube channel. One of the fantastic pieces of advice that she gave, was that you should write down 100 ideas of what you are going to talk about, before you start. The reasoning was that you need to (a). be sure that you want and need a channel, and (b) make sure that whilst you are starting it, you are not worried about running out

---

[xx] See, *Finishers & Completionists will kill us all*.

of ideas. It's fantastic advice.

So, surely I should do the same when I am writing this regular thing? When I started this, back in November 2019, I did have 3 pieces of work written. It certainly removed some of the stress, and allowed me to workout the *mechanics* of doing this. Now, that is not the case.

Sure, if at 3am I come up with 2 pieces, then I will write them. That is not my normal approach. In essence, by removing the pressure & stress of having to write something, I just *trust myself* that I will think of something and then write it.

Trusting myself to come up with an idea has been a wonderful release. It also means that hopefully these pieces are more *of the moment* rather than heavily scripted and staged.

"Hang on", I hear none of you saying, what about if you can't think of something. What do you do then?!

Oh that's easy, when I *can't think of something*, then I just write about the fact that *I can't think of something*.

Most of the time, I have no idea what I am doing. Recently, I have concluded, I'm actually totally OK with that; it's quite empowering, and I would recommend that *you give it a go* ...

My name is Nigel Derbyshire, and I have no idea what I am doing.

Creative

Just Thinking

Have you ever wondered, what it was like.

Have you ever wondered what the full moon would look like, if you did a handstand and looked at it upside down? Have you ever wondered what an ant's view of the world is, so have gotten down onto your belly in the pouring rain? Have you ever taken pots of black, blue & red ink, and sniffed each one in turn, just to see if they smell different? Have you ever spent 30 minutes winking at your dog, just to see if you could trick him into winking back?

Well, dear reader, I can tell you now ... that I've not done any of those things.

I have though, given some serious thought to each one. I have mused. I have thought about. I

Creative

have wondered.

I am one of those thinkers. A professional thinker-of-things. I spend an inordinate amount of time thinking about random junk. Why do we try and make butter spread like margarine, and try to make margarine taste more like butter?

So why? Why do I waste important brain-cycles on this kind of junk?

Quite simply, I do it because I can. Specifically, I see such tremendous value in *thinking*. I'm not talking about thinking about *something*, I am talking about thinking about *anything*.

There is a complete separation, at least in my mind, between *thinking* about something and *doing* something. With that firmly in place, my mind is free to wonder about ... what would happen if you took some play dough and mixed it with fire?

I know there are fine folk out there who are experimentalists, who would gladly amble into a craft store, and purchase some play-dough. Followed by some lighter-fluid. Followed by setting up a high-speed camera rig, to record the event (for YouTube consumption).

I used to think that I was one of those folk. Time has changed that view. Well actually, a basic

Just Thinking

lack of skill has changed that view.

As a result of a random set of events, I recently gained access to CERN.[xxi] It was all legal and above board, but it was a little unexpected. For those in the dark about CERN, it's the place with the large whizzy circular thing where they smash small things into other small things very fast, to see if they can recreate the Sun or the Universe. (Permit me some artistic license here).

Whilst logging into their fantastic systems, I was presented with a view of all of the departments at the location. It was mind blowing, with all of the obscure and obvious departments listed. In summary, again allow me some license here, they were grouped into; (a) Thinkers, (b) Doers, (c) Collectors.

Thinkers - Theoretical Physics. Doers - Experimental Physics. Collectors - Data Analysis.

So, that clearly puts me into the same category as Theoretical Physicists. Sure, we have different skills, but we are both thinking in the abstract. Sure, the output of their thoughts has a marginally wider consequence than mine, but I ask you, how

---

[xxi] Conseil Européen pour la Recherche Nucléaire. Now often referred to as the European Laboratory for Particle Physics.

many of them have seriously thought about play dough and fire!?

I'm sure there was a point I was trying to make here. Oh yes, and I guess that is the point.

I've written before about how Finishers & Completionists will kill us all[xxii]; this is in the same vein. There I was talking about the pursuit of, and potential completion of, tasks. Or rather the value of not doing that.

Here I'm applying the same idea, to one's thoughts.

I described myself as a "Startist", regarding tasks. I'm not sure what the mental, thought-based, sister of that is, but I'm that too.

What does this mean, and why does it even matter?

I'm not for one second going to suggest that my musing about play-dough-fire will produce anything remotely earth-changing. No, this one is more personal.

I was rubbish at maths. I'm still rubbish at maths. I just can't do it in my head. I can make machines do it for me, but I just don't have the

---

[xxii] See, *Finishers & Completionists will kill us all*.

plumbing in my head to do it all in there. As soon as I embark on a thought process that requires that particular skill, I have that knowing feeling of dread; I will fail.

There are other things that fall into that category too; lists. I know how to make them, just not in my head. I'm not talking about failing to hold 27 items in a virtual list in one's head. No, my item limit is 2 or 3. In fact, whenever I have to remember 2 things, I find myself worrying that I've forgotten the third item. I've certainly spent many a time walking up and down the aisles in a supermarket, trying desperately to recall what the third item was. Later to discover that there were only ever two items on the damn list! I now write every list down; even a list of one.

In both of those cases, the known possible failure causes stress.

With musing, there is none of that; there is no required outcome. No worrying problem, no need to get to a solution.

This kind of free-wheeling-thinking, is just like taking a skinny dip into a fresh springtime stream. Chilly at first, but a delightful sense of pure relaxation and calm.

I like that.

It turns out that I also need that. I need that kind of thought-oil, in my mind. It not only lubricates the more complex parts, it also seems to allow access to other creative parts. Those creative parts that were previously obscured by problem-solving-results-driven tasks.

I know that we can't spend all of our waking moments, thinking about play dough and fire. I do though, think that allowing yourself to meander along a thought-path with no intention of arriving anywhere, is remarkably valuable.

In a world that seems to be getting evermore complex, and rammed full of critically important problems, we should grab onto anything that frees up our minds. Grabbing hold of anything that lubricates our minds. Grabbing onto those chinks of magic that make us so very human, in thought.

It will help.

Collecting

It's not about the doing.

I love visiting the British Museum. Specifically, I love walking into the Enlightenment room. It's a place that is all about the Discovery that took place during the 18th century. It's got all sorts of wonderful stuff in there, including a copy of the Rosetta Stone.[xxiii]

As well as all of the main exhibits, there are stacks of books around the edge of the room. Giant books; old books; textured books; books. They are placed on dark wooden bookcases, with glass doors. I once asked, where the books had come from, and if there was a catalogue of all of them.

[xxiii] A 44 by 30 inch sized stone from 45BC, with an inscribed message in Greek & Hieroglyphs. It was key in deciphering the hieroglyphic code in 1822.

Creative

Apparently they are an overflow from the British Library, and that there is probably a catalogue somewhere. I got the distinct impression I was the first person to inquire for quite some time.

I love how the books seem to encase all of the knowledge on display.

I love books. I love them as wonderful objects. I love that they are packed full of knowledge, of adventure, of written imagination.

With my love of books, you would expect that I am an avid reader. That I consume books like a packet of biscuits.

I am not.

I just love books.

Now, I already know that I am a little odd, but I was somewhat reassured the other day on discovering that I am not alone. At least regarding my view of books.

Tsundoku[27] is the art / skill / obsession / complication, of acquiring reading materials and letting them pile up without reading them.

I had, at last, found my group-calling. I wasn't an outcast in the book world. I had friends, or perhaps inmates, who had the same passion as me.

Collecting

The Japanese word originated in the Meiji era (1868 - 1912) as slang. It now has a wider recognition, and indeed, avid following. It's a real thing, I can cast off my guilt. I'm part of a movement now, or is that a cult? Anyway, begone reading guilt; hello the warm embrace of *Tsundoku*.

Flushed with the success of finding an additional calling, I pondered if the same *essence* could be extracted and then applied to other things.

I am an avid collector of information, of data, of factoids, of brain content-enhancing matter, of brain-food.

I know the quickest time you can sharpen 10 pencils down to nothing by hand (around 40 minutes). I know how to cut a cake for 3 people in a way that everyone is equally happy with their slice. I know what happens when you take a Kalashnikov AK-47 & fire 700 rounds through it continuously. I know what happens when you add up 1+2+3+4+5+ ... to infinity.

I have no intention of using these pieces of knowledge. They just sit inside my brain. Occasionally I will pick one of them up, wonder at it a little, then carefully put it back.

There is often a social pressure to acquire

Creative
___

things so that you can do something *with them*. You are told to acquire books, so that you can read them. You are told to learn how to speak another language, so you can use it. You are told to acquire knowledge about something, so you can *learn* something.

How about just enjoying the *acquisition* and ignoring the *application*?

How about acquiring books or knowledge, without any intention whatsoever in reading or using?

Wouldn't that remove a certain amount of pressure? It does for me.

So, as soon as is practical, I'm going to go out and get some books that I just *like the look of*. In the mean time, I'm going to look at the notion that there are different *infinities* and that some are larger than others.

It really is relaxing and, I have to say, somewhat refreshing for the mind.

The Language of Words

Your self-representation.

I recently[xxiv] talked about how words seem to take on a mind of their own, and somehow seem to change after they have been written down. I was, of course, trying to explain away my rather skilful ability to put the wrong word in the wrong place.

It was all about *Word Salad*.

I use a specific piece of software to *do my writing*; Ulysses[xxv]. I've been using it for just over a couple of years now. Well, according the statistics that it obediently keeps, I've written down around

---

[xxiv] See. *Words are a funny ole thing.*
[xxv] I don't now, but that doesn't matter.

Creative

400,000 words. I'm not sure if that is a lot or not enough, but it got me to thinking about *why and what*.

In 1921 Ludwig Wittgenstein, a subsequent philosopher of note, published a work called *Tractatus*.[28] The ground-breaking work, stated that the limits of philosophy were tied to the limits of language. Further, that the limits of thought and expression of an individual, were also limited by language.

In essence, Wittgenstein is saying that our ability to think, express ourselves and to reason, are directly linked to and limited by our grasp of language.

In the same way in which *Time* could be considered one of the cornerstones of *Physics*, perhaps it follows that *words* could be considered the cornerstone of our *thinking selves*.

So, apparently all those words I've written down are actually quite important.

On 1st December 2015, I wrote this piece of poetry, titled "Filling page" (published in my book *Accidental Poetry*, in 2018)[29]

Letters from creative fingers of self; I learn the workings of my mind.

Patterns before me, filling downwards; help calm my thoughts.

A drizzle falls into words of meaning; but what?

With increasing numbers, comfort and creative calm; lubricating time.

White space battle black words; awkward grey results.

Moment passed, word misspelled, creative place explored; conclude.

Here I was expressing how the letters that spill from my creative thoughts, fall like drizzle onto the page, forming words. Collectively those words fill the page, into a creative work.

Later in the same book, I express the difficulties in finding words. Words seem to have a special ever present power.

Back in the early 2000s, someone wondered what would happen if you could video record every single moment of your life. Would it give some kind of overall expression, that you couldn't get from a single photograph. They got funding, and created a small device that you would wear like a neckless. It would take a snapshot every 30 seconds, continuously. Each night, those snapshots would be uploaded, and a time-lapse video would be created. In the theoretical laboratory, that seemed like a great idea; in real life, people valued their privacy.

In spite of its failure, it does make you wonder about the collective accumulation of images, and what that might show. In the present day, you could argue that we are close to that, in a combination of Twitter, Facebook & Instagram.

Does the same apply to words?

As you would expect by now, I was pondering that very thought.

There is a distinct difference between spoken words, and the written word. I think it's down to the fact that the spoken words are considered to be more transient in nature. I mean, who can actually remember exactly the words that they used on 11 July 1984 at 5:34pm?

The written word, is a little more considered. Perhaps that is because you need to, or rather should strive to, take into account grammar. With the spoken word, that seems to be a little more fluid; more artistic license is in play.

The written word, generally takes more mental effort to create. So perhaps that does give it a greater weight of importance.

The Languate of Words

Wittgenstein saw a link between language and thought.

When I think about something I hear a voice in my head. When I write something, I hear the same voice, but it is calmer and more considered in its tone. Perhaps because it is both formal and rigid, it is therefore a somewhat richer expression.

So, if I took everything I have ever written down as a whole, could that then, be an expression or at the very least a representation, of my *self*?

I'm not sure. I am sure though, that I should keep writing these words; they appear to be important.

Creative

Glue

It's more than you think it is.

We've all been there, exposed pipes. To be clear, I'm not talking about the bagpipe kind of problem. I'm talking about the complex situation around the presentation of water pipes.

The ability to safely transport water around a building, is a wonder. For myself, while I'm perfectly happy mucking around with electrical wiring; water pipes fill me with dread. Which is a little odd, when you think about it. Water leaking *over* your hands has a rather different outcome, than electricity leaking *into* your hands!

I have an admiration of those who have the skills, and indeed tools, to perform this modern-day miracle. Those demi-gods who work with gas, truly deserve some sort of plaque or something.

Creative

For me I just want to hide it all away. I'm perfectly happy to see a grubby electrical extension cable pushed down the back of a desk, but I just feel an overwhelming urge to cover up those fresh copper pipes.

It's not clear where all this comes from, as I know I'm not alone in this compulsion. Maybe it is as simple as this; permanent infrastructure, should be hidden. The grubby cable is viewed as a temporary *hack*, which makes it more socially acceptable. I don't know, but having your pipes on display is a social faux-pas.

The options available are clear. 1. Paint. 2. Boxed way. 3. Fabric. Lets take each one in turn. The first is the obvious choice. Make the tubular creations part of the wall texture. That connection being made by using the same colour paint. This sensible approach soon runs into a texture problem of it own, when the pipes are a mixture of metal and plastic; paint just doesn't adhere to them both in the same way. So, it looks like a mess. Attack number 2 is your get-out-of-jail card here. Although requiring more skill (than I have), it can look rather fetching once complete. There is though, dear reader, a scenario where neither 1 nor 2 will be able to resolve; wash-hand basins.

I give you, a small wash-hand basin with a mix-

Glue

ture of copper and plastic pipes twisted together, set tightly into the corner of a small room. What to be done?

Obviously it can't be left. I mean, it starts with you telling yourself that it will be OK, that you will get used to it. But no, as those three weeks amble past it just starts to grate. Something needs to be done.

Over some overly lengthy, and somewhat easily distractable, online investigation, a solution is devised. I give you, *operation fabric*. You may know it as it's more informal name, a curtain. With suitable choice of fabric, it will resolve the matter and can also act as a statement art piece.

With fabric chosen, we get to the seemingly straight forward part; fitting and connection. Bringing us to the point I wanted to make; glue.

Having exhausted all other kinds of sticky-back hooks, as just not being up to the task, we must once again lean on our friend, glue. In a cunning plan involving a knife and some not-so-careful scraping of the back of the hooks, we are ready.

The glue didn't work. Something about porcelain, wood-glue, and plastic, not being happy bedfellows. The porcelain and the plastic were non-negotiable parties, it must be the glue.

Creative

Hunting through old desk drawers, ordering random stuff online, and eventually a happy partnership seems to have been found. It was whilst introducing these new friends together, that the *event* occurred.

From a young age, it was drummed into us, that you never ever get super-glue on your skin. At all costs.

I saw the drip of glue fall from the edge of the basin. Like a small droplet of water, it moved ever closer towards my trousers. I didn't try to catch it, I didn't try to stop it (for which I awarded myself bonus points). Finishing the job in had, it was time for inspection. No damage to me, just a small circular dark mark, on my trouser leg.

Numerous washes haven't removed it in anyway; it was here to stay. Which got me thinking.

The glue had stopped being the *thing* that connected one thing to another. It had become *it's own self*.

Glue gets a bad wrap. It is viewed as a necessary tool, and a tool of last of resort. It is never, if rarely, seen in it's own right.

So what does this all mean, and why has it taking me so long to get to the point?

Glue

As we go through life, we are always trying to get from A-to-B. Trying to get person A to talk to person B. Trying to turn object A into object B. Trying to change an emotion from A to B. In essence, that *trying* looks a lot like glue. Taking two *things* and trying to transform them into something else. Some put more effort into this *trying* than others, but we all do it.

I guess, what I am saying is, that just like the glue we rarely think of the act of *trying* to be something in it's own right. We fail to attached the *act of trying* itself as a *thing*. In not doing so, we can label the trying-act as *effort*.

Viewing *effort*, *trying*, *glue*, as single distinct things, allows us to appreciate them on their own terms. In doing so, these in-between things move from obstacles to items. That my help reduce their stress association.

Creative

Scrolling Entertainment

A meander through cheese, pickled onions & electronic glass.

From when I was a kid, in the 1970s, I have many clear memories, some sketchy ones, and some that I just can't remember. Most of those during that time, are completely irrelevant to what I am chatting about today; we will just gleefully skip past them.

Anyway, as I navigate through the slightly less than catalogued memories, there is one that stands out clear. It was in our home in Norfolk, sitting crossed legged on the floor around a small round table. Said table is still in operation today, although my ability to sit crossed legged under it

Creative

is not.

The table has a crocheted cream cloth on it, again still in operation, and had on it what we used to call a "dry tea".

It wasn't until much later, that it became clear to me that the term "dry tea" is a somewhat "unique" phrase. Nowadays, and probably then too, the more mainstream term would be a "small buffet". There are two things on that table that I vividly remember; cubes of strong cheddar cheese, and homemade pickled onions.

Those two items still play an important role in my life, today.

I feel I need to take a moment, call it a moment of respect if you like, to briefly chat about those food items in question.

Growing up in the middle of Norfolk was lovely, the default entertainment consisted of the arrival of the weekly bus, on Tuesday I think, and walking the fields collecting interesting looking stones. One of the additional adventures, was the monthly shop. It entailed a lengthy adventure to travel all the way to the city of Norwich, to visit the Sainsbury's supermarket. Our connection with Sainsbury's goes all the way back to Muswell Hill in London, and the nearby Sainsbury's shop where they used to hand-prepare the butter using butter paddles. So, we were a "Sainsbury's family", and still are to this day.

Where was I? Oh yes, back to the cheese. After the massive adventure of the tiny country roads, the metal black & white World War 2 road signs that could be moved around to "fool the Germans", we would arrive at Sainsbury's.

We would have two trolleys, one that would be filled with bread, and another with other stuff. I have a vivid memory of Mum going to the cheese counter, and asking for some cheese. She pointed, through the glass, to a giant block of strong cheddar cheese. The helpful assistant, I'm not sure if cheese assistants have a special name, asked "how much". Mum looked at them and said, "No, that block. All of it." We were a cheese family.

The other food item in question, was the pickled onion. My Great Grandmother, who was given the title of "Nanny Billings", had many skills. One of which was the magical creation of "picked onions". They would be made in giant jars, rammed full of spices, and the kept in a small dark cupboard under the stairs. I was never quite sure how long they were left to mature, but in my kid's eye view of the world, it was surely decades.

Creative

My first foray into the world of pickled onions was, I am told, when I was 2 years old. I got hold of a large pickled onion and took a giant bite out of it. It was so strong, that it made me cry. After the crying had subsided, I asked for some more. The dye had been cast; I was a pickled onion lover from that milestone forward.

OK, I realise that I have wandered so far off the reservation of what I was actually going to talk about, that we might actually need a rather expensive Garmin[30] waterproof handheld GPS unit[xxvi], to get back to it.

Note to self; perhaps I should write articles that are just giant preambles.

Back to the small table with cheese, and pickled onions.

This was not a guest-social event; this was a Saturday evening event. The event in question was Dr Who on BBC1. Specially Tom Baker's Dr Who.

We would sit around the table, allowing us to get a little closer to the Cathode Ray Tube display unit, and watch Dr Who. It was utterly delightful, and if, by some random course of events, Tom

---

[xxvi] Garmin GPSMap 60CSx.

Scrolling Entertainment

Baker should ever read this, then I would like to say "Thank You".

It was, as I hope you can see, an event. It was an entertainment event.

Throughout my childhood, there were a number of similar entertainment events. Morecombe & Wise; James Bond films ... you get the picture.

As we project forwards, those events became less defined. The event itself was in many ways greater, but the setting of the event became less defined. I can clearly remember the episode on 21 March 1981, where Tom Baker faded into Peter Davison. I cannot though, remember the external setting in which that took place. I have a memory of the thing, but not what I was eating or doing at the time. I have no memory of cheese and pickled onion sandwiches, at that particular tele-visual event.

Over the coming years, there was a clear migration away from the setting of the entertainment event as being important, and a move towards the importance of the event itself.

I think this was linked to the accessibility of the event itself. As the effort of accessing the event decreased, the importance of the setting where you consumed the event also decreased.

Creative

I am sitting in an Italian restaurant, as I write this piece. As I glance around, I can see a slice of our current humanity. Sure there is plenty of chatter and social engagement, but there is also a certain amount of "phone-scrolling".

Don't get me wrong, it is not intrusive or inappropriate. No, it covers those micro-moments between conversation, or those moments when then other-half wanders off to "spend a penny".

On the graph of accessibility of entertainment vs effort, the dotted line has projected so far way from effort, as to have smudged off the piece of paper and is currently making a mark on the table.

As I started this article, the memory was about the setting of the entertainment. Why? Because the effort required to witness the said entertainment was significant; it deserved an appropriate corresponding setting event.

As I write this in 2020, the graph has moved so far away from that initial social context, as to have created something rather different.

It would seem that the actual "accessibility of entertainment" has overtaken the entertainment itself. It seems like a natural projection.

The ease of which you can access an entertain-

Scrolling Entertainment

ment item itself, has overtaken the entertainment itself, in terms of social value.

Indeed I would say, as I sit in this restaurant, that the process of scrolling has itself become the source of entertainment.

The brutal indirect creativity of humanity has created a wondrous new form of entertainment. Welcome to Scrolling Entertainment. With no cheese, no pickled onions, and no round table. Just you, your thumb and a piece of electronic glass.

Creative

Whimsical Thinking

We all need a little fun. How about letting your mind meander off on that interesting footpath of fun creativity.

I do like having a bit of whimsical fun. There is something very freeing about letting your mind wander off a path, and into the dense undergrowth, whilst of coarse holding a blue umbrella and wearing flip-flops that are 3 sizes too small.

Whimsical

Magical Pie

We need to talk about pie.

I've been feeling, for some time now, that I should be writing something about Pie. I'm just not sure what.

I have a complicated relationship with Pie. My problem is, that they are invisible.

Now, I'm not saying that they are *invisible* in a Harry Potter kind of way (although that would be groovy-cool). No, what I am talking about is fiendishly more twisted than that.

For those of you who have read The Hitchhiker's Guide to the Galaxy,[31] there is a concept called an S-E-P. In the scenario described, a spaceship lands in the middle of London, and not a single person notices it. The reason? It has an S-E-P cloak. Something so powerful that it renders it invisible; *Somebody Else's Problem.*

The illusion of invisibility works by exploiting a flaw in the human psyche. Namely, that ability to totally ignore something that is none of their business or concern. The British are world leaders at this. The S-E-P cloak remotely amplifies this *skill* and hey-presto, *invisibility*.

Back to Pie. I have a suspicion that something vaguely similar is going on with Pie.

When I open the fridge, and glance in to see what there is to cook, I can honestly say that I have never noticed the absence of a Pie; I have never thought, "wish I had some Pie". It just doesn't happen.

However, if there is a Pie in the fridge, then I will almost always choose that. Even if I have eaten one the day before. Odd.

The oddity continues when I go food shopping. I can't ever really remember ambling around and randomly deciding to buy a Pie. I mean I have, on occasion, specifically purchased a Pie, as the result of having it written on an actual physical scrap of paper. Just never *accidentally*.

Now this can't be said for other food items;

Magical Pie

I have lost count of the number of Scotch Eggs, Olives, bottles of Red Wine, packets of Crisps, that I have *accidentally* purchased. Just not Pie.

What does this mean? Should you care? Does the Government need to launch a cross-department tax-payer funded investigation into it?

Well, I do think that there are questions to be answered, not least of which; how does Pie get into my house if I don't purchase it?

As you would expect, I have been giving this some considerable thought. I have deployed all of the skills I have obtained from episodes of Morse, Lewis, Elementary & Sesame Street.

You will, dear reader, be glad to know that I have some answers for you. Even if you don't actually like Pie, or care about it, then you will at least be grateful that this rambling word-river will shortly conclude into a rather disappointingly average lake.

My conclusion is that, *Pies are like Clouds.*

Perhaps I should expand on that a little. We all seem to notice the sunshine, and the rain, but how often do we notice the Clouds? Sure, if you are proactively looking at the Clouds, then you will notice them. But, how often have you stepped out

Whimsical

of your home and muttered, "what an entirely averagely and uniformly grey cloud-day it is." We do however say, "lovely sunshine", and "crappy rain".

If you actually take some time out of your day, lay on your back (outside obviously), and look up into the sky, then Clouds can be wondrous. They are a captivating visual treat.

I believe Pies hold the same quality. I may never remember buying them, I may never accidentally purchase them, I may never long after them when presented with a sparse fridge. But. Eating a good Pie, is a magical experience.

The magic is perhaps tied up in their invisibility, perhaps it is because they are just so unassuming. They are the grey-clouds, that can deliver your food in edible packaging, self-contained goodness, filling, warm, with an often slight crisp to its crust.

The humble Pie is, I conclude, a mystical beast that appears from nowhere, leaves a momentary delight, then disappears into the ether... until the next time.

I hope you can find time, to give a Pie a special moment. We all need a little magic in our lives, and what better way than to consume it in the form of a *Magical Pie*.

English Breakfast

Its omnipresence, is a lesson for us all.

The other day I had a full English Breakfast.

Well, when I say "full" that isn't quite true; it was missing the grilled tomato & the black pudding. For the record, 3 fried eggs, 2 sausages, 2 hash browns, 2 slices of brown buttered toast, baked beans, mushrooms, and 3 rashers of bacon (so crispy, that they could be used as a weapon). The rationale regarding the missing items, is that I don't think fruit should be cooked, and I don't like the idea of eating a "pudding" who's main ingredient is blood. The blood thing is a little odd, I have to admit. I would gladly consume bone marrow, and liver pate. Perhaps it's down to the fact that I have seen my own blood and not my own bone marrow or liver.

It was paired with a pot of Earl Grey tea, with lemon & not milk; I'm not an animal.

As predicted by myself, it was delightful.

Afterwards I was pondering, which is all you are capable of doing having eaten such a large breakfast. I recalled all the places I have eaten an English Breakfast. Obviously in multiple locations within the United Kingdom, but also in multiple countries around the World. Regarding the UK incidents, almost all of those were in hotels. There seems to be an unwritten rule that when in a hotel, you are duty bound to order an *English Breakfast* for breakfast. Sure, there is the "continental" breakfast, but to be brutally honest, you are viewed as a cheap-skate if you pursue that particular option.

Regarding the other worldwide locations, they were equally lovely, although on occasion it would be fair to describe them as "best efforts". I mean in Thailand, Lincolnshire sausages are a little light on the ground. Although the eggs were extra special.

If you are wondering where this discussion on English Breakfasts is going, then I can assure you, you are not alone.

I like the notion that there is a meal that has a

special status. I'm not saying that it is in anyway *better* than other meals. I would for example say that a medium rare fillet steak with bone marrow (still in the bone), is far better. But I think we can agree that it certainly has a special status. Wherever you are, if you ask for a *Full English Breakfast* there is a basic understanding as to what that entails. Sure, there are *interpretations*, but the essence is there. It is an omnipresent dish.

As we travel through our lives, we participate in a ride that is enjoyable, scary, full of twists and turns, but it is a ride that we are on whether we like it or not.

As I sit in this location, writing this, my behaviour and interaction with others is most definitely influenced by the surroundings. The social setting creates an appropriate number of boundaries and social norms. In general those norms are helpful. That is though, not always the case. In other settings, these conventions are in place to manipulate and control you. In the worst setting, they are in place to pro-actively discriminate against whole groups of people.

This social pressure to conform, or adjust ourselves, can be helpful but often create a negative force of change. We are passively manipulated into changing our behaviour to match it. This

Whimsical

low-level continuous action, coerces our psyche.

In essence our location and social setting, starts to define us. If you participate in a social group, this can actually help to oil the wheels of interaction. What happens though, if you are extracted from that group and find yourself on your own?

Something that I have given far too much thought to, is this. If I was standing in a field, (I tend to choose a field of wheat on a delightful summer afternoon with fluffy clouds gliding across a cyan-blue sky), then who am I?

Specifically, do I have a sense of my own identity. Can I define myself without reference to others?

To be sure, this isn't a mediatory requirement, but I do believe that it is an indicator as to your positive mental health.

Having a sense of your own identity leads to a sense of your own self-worth. This can inform the way that you choose to interact with others, but it can also act as a kind of default position; a point of reference.

If you take a plate and add the following items to it, 3 fried eggs, 2 sausages, 2 hash browns, 2

English Breakfast

slices of brown buttered toast, baked beans, mushrooms, and 3 rashers of bacon (so crispy, that they could be used as a weapon); you have an English Breakfast.

If you go into a hotel in Singapore and ask for an English Breakfast, you will get a close approximation of that.

It is, in essence, a universal dish.

The definition of the English Breakfast, isn't determined by its location or social setting. It is defined by its ingredients. An English Breakfast in America, isn't a salmon omelette with avocado.

As we look at ourselves, we often define ourselves by our location and social setting. On one level that is helpful, but on a deeper level, I don't believe it is helpful; if that setting changes or disappears, then we can be lost.

My dear readers, in conclusion, if we want to be mentally healthy, we should perhaps view ourselves as English Breakfasts.

Whimsical

Words are a funny ole thing

I am just leasing these words from the language.

Words, are a strange beast. Even once they are written, they seem to squirm and wriggle around. I've often written words that are in a perfect line, only to come back later to discover that they have changed order and are now a rather fetching curve!

I guess it's just a law of nature, or physics, or Murphy's law, or just a random event that looks like it isn't random?

Word Salad. Somewhat surprisingly it is actually a medical term, although don't quote me on that. It describes the notion of a Salad of Words.

That is to say, you generally know what a Salad looks like and should taste like, as a whole. By the way, I'm talking about vanilla salad here, not the stuff with crunchy croutons in. I'm also not saying that vanilla salad actually tastes at all like vanilla. Anyway, you get the idea that as a whole you know what a bowl of Salad looks like and generally should taste like. Trouble is, if you pick out various bits, say the lettuce part, is it Iceberg lettuce or Little Gem lettuce? It can be hard to determine. Same with the tomatoes, are they (I don't actually know much about tomatoes, so just pretend that I've made a similar comparison).

So Word Salad is that, but with words. It's like you know the overall sense (flavour) of the word, but you just can't seem to grasp the exactness of it. I have this, although rather curiously only with speech.

I will be chatting away, then suddenly I don't know what the next word is. I have an emotional sense of what it is, but I just can't seem to find it (in the Salad of Words). After a period of socially awkward time, I will either have found it, or will engineer my way around it, and have chosen another word that has a similar feel. Or just say that I have Word Salad and abandon the whole sentence. The latter course of action can be somewhat offset by a humours anecdote about Word Salad.

I have always had a fascination with language. I'm sure you are expecting me to list all of the interesting and novel languages that I speak; I can only speak English. Not sure why that is, perhaps it is just down to a lack of effort on my part, and a lack of need on my part.

Italian would be first on my list, probably followed by Japanese, then Icelandic. The final choice might surprise you, but I'm just being practical here.

One of the languages that I have an interest in, is Old English. It was in use from around 450AD to 1150AD, so around 700 years during the Anglo-Saxon times in England. Whilst there are some written forms of it, no one speaks it anymore. The sound and flow of the language has essentially been lost.

Around 5 years ago, I stumbled upon a video on YouTube from 2008, where Alexander Arguelles[32] translates and then reads some Old English. Written down, it seems very strange whereby it feels like you should be able to read it but that you just can't seem to. Spoken it sounds really odd and other-worldly. It kind of sounds like each word is being read backwards, but does have a wonderful melodic odd charm to it. At the end of the video he says, as if in passing, that if you want to have a chance of tackling Old English then you should first learn Icelandic. Hence my choice.

Other word and language examples are from the current favourite game, Animal Crossing. In the game you control a little character who lives on an island. They interact with lots of other independent characters, and between yourselves you can build up a cute island with lots of stuff on it. It truly is an original and wonderful game; highly recommended. In the game the characters need to talk to each other. You get speech bubbles appear when the do. The problem for the game creators, is that they needed a language-sound when that happened. There have been a number of these games in the series over the years, that all have this requirement. Being sold all over the world, the cost of voice acting and translating would be prohibitively expensive. So, they invented a non-language sound. It sounds like they are talking, but it is actually just gibberish[xxvii]. Imagine my surprise when I found out from Jenna Stoeber,[33] that the English and Japanese versions of the game

---

[xxvii] See, *The Gibberish of Rhubarb*.

Words are a funny ole thing

had different gibberish sounds!

Back to these words. I'm sure you have seen examples from previous editions where the words have re-formed into something else. Sometimes individual words seem to entirely, well disappear. It seems to be out of my control. Indeed, this same fate may have been dealt to his body of words too.

In conclusion, we all know that English has its only curious oddities. I will leave you with this little gem. It relates to the something that was drilled into me at school; *I before E except after C.*

I before E except when your *feisty foreign neighbour Keith leisurely receives eight counterfeit beige sleighs from caffeinated atheist weightlifters; weird.*

Whimsical

The Jelly & Marshmallow Wars

The untold buttery war.

I started writing this for a number of reasons. Mostly health related, but also to see if I actually could. I'll leave you to be a judge of my output, but I appear to have been able to continue; even if it is the only thing I'm able to achieve in a given week.

Anyway, this morning I was considering what it has been like to have such a forced creative task each week. I recognise that it is way less than most of you probably have to deal with, but I'm still going to talk about it.

Some weeks, it flows like a creatively oiled machine.

Some weeks, it could best be described as collecting jelly, using marshmallow hands, and having caught the jelly then needing to balance it on a hot plate, whilst sculpting it using a butter covered spoon.

Which got me thinking about the, oft undocumented, *Jelly & Marshmallow Wars*.

I'm sure you've heard of it. Although in recent years, and might I say for politically motivated reasons, the topic seems to have been dropped from the education syllabus.

Like most things, it all started in 2000 BC; around 4000 years ago. A young apprentice food scientist, although to be historically accurate we should refer to him as a cook, was taking an afternoon break. Again, if we are going to be pedantically historically accurate, he had been working since 2am and the break was more enforced rather than suggested. He was taking a walk along his usual route, although the records do show that he was actually a she, and that she was of slightly higher rank than a mere cook. Anyway, Chef Lisa, sorry I've made up her name; it's not recorded. She was taking a stroll.

It was a stroll along her favourite route. Her

stroll started in North Africa, and stayed in North Africa, because it was just a stroll. As was usual, Lisa loved taking a route down into the lower more shaded area of the town. It's not known which town it actually was, but it was known that it had a more shaded area. Pausing to ponder her chosen career choices, Lisa noticed a small green plant with a delicate white flower. It was of course *Althaea officinalis*, a common plant in the marshy areas. Her motivation is unknown, perhaps in wonder, perhaps out of curiosity, perhaps out of rage at the long hours she was being forced to work. She gently plucked, pulled, ripped, the historical records are unclear as to which, the plant from the ground. In doing so, part of the stem snapped off in her hand. Thinking nothing of it, she looked at the sweet white five-petalled flower, and then discarded the plant.

It was later that afternoon, whilst butchering a small animal, that she noticed her left hand was sticky. Specifically the area between her thumb and index finger. Remembering that she had forgotten to wash her hands before starting on the butchery, and the plant incident, she made a mental note.

The next day, that mental note was recalled, and she revisited the same location. Thankfully

Whimsical

for us, more of the plants were present. Breaking the stem open, she discovered the white fleshy and slightly sticky core. Remembering what a dog's breakfast the butchery turned out to be, she decided that she could use this white sticky substance for something. She needed a name for it, something that would give it some presence and earn her some much needed kudos. Her name was Lisa Mestowa, and so the name was set.

Having collected a number of the plants, she returned to the kitchen area to present her findings to the head chef. The Mestowa plant, and more specially the recipe of boiling it with honey and straining it, was presented. The head chef, who's name is sadly, or luckily for them, lost in time, took a moment. Surprised at Lisa's calm persona, she was quizzed further. She expressed her genuine feeling of being relaxed and mellow, and disclosed that she had found the plant over the ridge, in the shaded area, next to the marsh.

And so after meeting with others, and in a deliberate move to take all the credit, the head chef declared that the new discovery and food, be called the *marsh-mellow*.

In 1592, Prospero Alpini[34] documented these historical events. He was known for his terrible handwriting, and so the *marshmallow* was created.

The Jelly & Mashmallow Wars

It took until the late 1800s, when some France confectioners used the plant to create a candy called *Pate de Guimauve*.[35] Taking two days to make, it was a distinct delicacy.

The humble plant remained in use, until some bright spark in 1956 realised that you could make the same *kind of thing* from sugar and starch. So, the mass-produced candy that we know today was created.

To this day, Lisa is still not credited as the originator.

So, what about Jelly?

That was created in 1740 by a guy called Bob, who had some calf's feet and wondered if he could sell them. No one wanted calf's feet, so he boiled them and noticed a gelatinous substance left over. He discarded the bones and sold the substance as *calf's foot jelly*. In 1747, *Hannah Glasse* sensibly dropped the calf reference. And in her ground breaking book, The Art of Cookery[36] on page 285, created the a trifle with a layer of *jelly*.

I have to confess that there was no war at all, but I needed to hook you in. If for no reason than to highlight the dis-service dished out to Lisa.

In reality it really just boils down to the fact

Whimsical

that *Marshmallow* and *Jelly* are wobbly, and both equally difficult to sculpt with a *buttery* spoon.

The Gibberish of Rhubarb

The long game.

We often hear it. We often speak. We often refer to it. I am, of course talking about Pineapple.

In many ways, Pineapple is the new Rhubarb. Rhubarb's unique party trick, was that if you cooked it in the form of a Rhubarb crumble, then ate too much of it, it would make your teeth soft and your tongue numb. That particular mantel has now been passed to the rather alien-shaped Pineapple. It's party piece is to skilfully segment the population into "yes-please" and "are-you-joking". The Pineapple attack on the Rhubarb, started in the 1970s. The migration from a mere canned product, into something that can be cooked upside-down, was a master stroke. Rhubarb, on the other hand, thought that its toxic leaves would be enough to stave off this upstart. It was, alas, not enough. The raging success of the Pineapple-pizza marketing ploy, was the final blow. Not content with a mere success in overthrowing Rhubarb, Pineapple went in for the kill.

Some say that the promise was an everlasting supply of Pineapple, others speculate that it was a promise to root out all of the Rhubarb in the Country. We will never know. The year was 2017, the month was February, the place was the noble country of Iceland. As reported by Robin Pogrebin, in the New York Times,[37] no less than the President of Iceland, Gudni Thorlacius Johannesson, stated; "... *if I had the powers, I would pass a law banning pineapple on pizza ...*".

This sparked an international out-cry and predictable outrage online, which forced the President to backtrack with this formal statement;

"I like pineapples, just not on pizza. I do not have the power to make laws which forbid people to put pineapples on their pizza. I am glad that I do not hold such power. Presidents should not have unlimited power. I would not want to hold this position if I could pass laws forbidding that which I don't like. I would not want to

live in such a country. For pizzas, I recommend seafood."

The recommendation of seafood, didn't help to conclude the matter.

Widely regarded as a master move on the Pineapple's front, this anti-news distilled the food-loving public into one camp or the other.

Everyone was talking about Pineapple. Everyone had forgotten about Rhubarb. The fruit-flavoured bloody battle, had reached its nasty conclusion. Pineapple, was king.

Across the United Kingdom, unattended Rhubarb was left to fend for itself. It looked like there was no way back. Pineapple with its new-money, looked to have taken an unassailable lead.

It was not, however, the end of the matter.

You should never underestimate a vegetable with poisonous leaves. You should never ignore a vegetable that can be eaten with fruit.

As those vast unkept leaves shielded the core from the blazing sun, the pieces of a plan started to fall into place.

It was a long-game plan, that was so long, it was sown back in the 16th century. So devious in its very nature, so vast in scale, as to be the stuff

Whimsical

of future-legend.

For the Rhubarb, used throughout China for thousands of years, knew that as it gently moved outwards into medieval Arabia and then into Europe; it knew, that such a time would come.

With as much speed as a root vegetable can muster, a left-field multi-purpose plan was put into place.

Masterful plans need a time and a place. The time was the early 16th century. The place was England. However, effective plans need partners. They need willing parties to, if necessary, lay down their lives. Rhubarb found such noble and willing folk. Noble of mind, but simple in stature;

"Jabber" and "Gibber".

Individual souls; the first talks quickly, the second mutters incoherently.

But, Rhubarb needed to meld them into something new. Something that would stand the test of time.

It is unknown what the payment actually was, the details lost in the mists of time, but a deal was struck.

"Gibberish"

The Gibberish of Rhubarb

A magical word, that sounded like it had existed forever. Hidden in an evolving English language. So instinctively understood, but which would require a whole paragraph to tightly define.

And there it sat, waiting. Listening for that moment. For that instruction from its master, Rhubarb.

Pineapple arrived soon after, ignorant and flamboyant. Rhubarb remained quiet.

It was a dangerous tactic. With Pineapple gaining traction in the 1820s; was the danger too much to bare? The flamboyant extravagance of Pineapple's move into the elite's households, required a small course correction from Rhubarb.

Transitioning from a vegetable into Pineapple's pudding world, corrected the course for Rhubarb.

As predicted, the response from Pineapple was as overly confident as its sharp leaves. The fatal error, so often made; rapid expansion. Now at an eye watering 28 million units per year, Pineapple had gone big!

Rhubarb had seen it coming. And when Pineapple had played the upside-down card, Rhubarb started its own final multi-decade play.

Whimsical

It knew Pineapple would pull ahead, although it still isn't clear how Pineapple moved into the pizza scene. Some say that it was a deal done by Rhubarb in a dark alley with an American unnamed organisation. Whatever happened, it provided the nudge.

It was a needed nudge; a required distraction. A distraction from a tiny seed that Rhubarb planted in 1980.

It was to be a gamble. The events of 1969, looked hopeful. Just a year after the final act was put into play, the year of 1981 proved the timing was perfect.

No one had a clue, no one would could see it; Rhubarb was starting to build its own momentum.

As Rhubarb had predicted, 2005 signalled that it was time to give Pineapple one final nudge.

The nudge needed to be in the limelight, for that limelight was getting brighter and more intense. Pizza was everywhere and Pineapple was always close by. Pineapple had also foolishly gained an emoji; greater fame.

In 2012, Rhubarb started secret negotiations with Iceland. Knowing that the 2008 financial crash, that Rhubarb had engineered, cost Iceland

The Gibberish of Rhubarb

dearly. It knew they would be "pliable".

The year was set, 2017. Rhubarb needed a flash in the plan to finally blind Pineapple to what was really going on.

It happened; Rhubarb made its final play.

What was that final play? What was the culmination of a 400 year long plan?

Pineapple had reached its multi-million unit, internationally recognised, maximum exposure, high point. Rhubarb had made sure of that.

But what of Rhubarb?

Thousands of years ago, it was a poisonous plant. In the 16th century it moved into Europe. Throughout the 18th & 19th century, this vegetable moved into the fruit pudding market. In 1969 the pre-internet started. In 1981 the Internet was born. In 2005 YouTube was born.

In 1980, Eric Sykes decided to make a short 28 minute film. In 2020, you can find it on YouTube; search for "Rhubarb, 1980".

When writing the script, Eric Sykes didn't notice that Rhubarb was his muse. You see, every single word in the entire script is the word "Rhubarb".

Whimsical

Rhubarb from poisonous plant, to medicine, to edible vegetable, to fruit pudding, to Comedy.

Comedy, you see, lives for ever.

Pineapple? Yeah ... that's still just a piece of fruit.

A Conclusion

So, what does this all mean? What is the point of it all? Have we actually learnt anything? Have we just wasted our time on all these words? Not sure.

I did though, want to finish on this recent piece. It somehow seems an appropriate conclusion to all of these words.

Conclusion

No one is looking; no one is listening

Create with abandonment, not with measurement.

The point in history, June 1883. The place, the magazine *The Chautauquan*[38] "If a tree were to fall on an island where there were no human beings would there be any sound?"

Well dear reader, I can almost hear the tension in your eyes. I've only just started and am I about to launch into a discussion, nay, a dissection of those very words, from a Metaphysical viewpoint? Surely it would be remiss of me, not to mention the 18th century philosopher George Berkeley? Perhaps if not by name, then by exploring the subjective idealism, of the statement? Well

Conclusion

then, perhaps we should take a moment to explore Albert Einstein's physics-based response to that very same, almost poetically expressed, moment of prose?

Of course we're not; you know me better than that. No, we are not even going to talk about trees. Nope, somewhat obviously, I am going to talk about Instagram.[39]

It's all about the clicks; the clicks on the 'gram. I'm not a big poster myself, I'm more of a consumer of its content. I am an avid clicker though. Scroll, double tap, scroll, repeat endlessly until you run out of time or your boss shouts at you. The double tap assigns a heart/like to the square image. It is a micro confirmation, that the image is "worthy". The greater the number that the image receives, obviously the better.

It's not much of a leap to imagine the post-reward-stress-check loop-trap, is in play here. There are people who will *delete posts*, if they don't get what they think is an appropriate level of "worth". It's a real problem.

But, that isn't what I want to talk about.

Think for a moment, of the photo itself. Specifically, the *worth-value* of that photo... just before it's posted on the 'gram? By the measure we have expressed above, it surely should have a worth-value of zero; no clicks yet.

Mmm, that doesn't feel right does it? I mean, you have already decided to post it, so it must have *some* value. Perhaps it is a different, lesser *type-value* measurement. Perhaps it has a "value" beforehand, that is then *overridden* once it appears online? Yes, that must be it.

Let's see if that works, with words.

Well yes, it does. For me, the process of creating words goes something like this. 1 - I think of something random, as described in my piece Creative Place[xxviii]. 2 - Start writing it. 3 - Hope that as I am writing it, the conclusion will present itself before I run out of words. 4 - Format & share.

At 12 noon on every Tuesday, it is freshly delivered to you. Then starts a rather frantic pressing of the refresh button by me, to see if anyone is actually bothered to open and read it. After 25 hours, I get an automated email detailing the stats.

It's kind of stressful.

Do you can see how the create-post-reward loop is similar, to the 'gram.

[xxviii] See, *Creative Place*.

Conclusion

Surely that is just a do-reward loop. We all know they are a good thing? I mean that is how you teach a dog (of any age) to do tricks.

If the tree falls in a forest, and no one is around to hear it, does it make a sound?

If I took a photo, and no one, and I mean not another living soul, ever saw it ... Or I wrote some words, and no one ever read them ...

What value is placed in those examples? The value placed on the photo before it is posted to the 'gram, is based on the *intent to post*. It's different but it is based on the *potential* action. The same pattern works for a body of words.

What happens if there is no intent, and no audience? Does that mean that the photo or words have *no value*?

That doesn't sound right to me. It *feels* like it does have a value. That value measurement, is not based on a potential or actual audience. It is based on an *internal*, my eyes only, proposition. We instinctively know this.

Why do people *delete* photos and words, that don't have a high enough *worth-value*?

The answer to the question, about the tree falling, and does it make a sound? ... The answer is actually *No*. It does not make a sound.

You see, sound *relies* on having an *audience*. It is an expression of the effect of someone *hearing it*. No *someone*, no *sound*.

Hang on though, the tree does still fall? I mean we are surely not suggesting that just because the tree doesn't have a sound, that the tree doesn't actually fall?

Of course we aren't saying that! The tree most definitely *does fall*.

Nigel, I'm getting confused about all this. It all sounds dangerously close to metaphysics, and you said that we weren't going to talk about that ... !

OK, deep breath; I'm almost out of words.

Measuring a falling tree purely by the *sound it makes*, is just as absurd as *measuring* a photo *just* by the size of its audience. The tree still falls; the photo is still taken.

We spend an awful lot of our time pausing, hesitating, stopping, from doing creative things before we have even started them. Based on the *perceived* audience value. Based on the *other-people* value. Based on the *approval* of others. We are constantly using that kind of measurement.

Conclusion

The tree is still a fallen tree. Your creative expression, is still *your expression*. The fallen tree, and your expression, are both independent of their external measurement.

Stop worrying and measuring. The only true measurement for *your creative expression*, is that *inward sense*. That internal wonderment. The pure sense of *self-worth*, of creating something.

This body of words exists, even if no one ever reads it. I kind of like the purity of that.

Bibliography

Articles and Books

[2] J. Venn. "On the employment of geometrical diagrams for the sensible representations of logical propositions". In: *Proceedings of the Cambridge Philosophical Society* 4 (1880), pp. 47–59 (cit. on p. 18).

[5] Helen Barolini. *Aldus & His Dream Book: An Illustrated Essay*. New York Italica Press, 2008. isbn: 978-0934977227 (cit. on p. 42).

[6] Lynne Truss. *Eats, Shoots & Leaves*. HarperCollins, 2009, p. 111. isbn: 9780007329069 (cit. on p. 42).

[7] Nicholas Humez Alexander Humez. *On the Dot: The Speck That Changed the World*. Oxford University Press USA, 2008. isbn: 978-0195324990 (cit. on p. 42).

[8] Nigel Derbyshire. *Mindful Cornucopia*. Carbon Writer, 2019. isbn: 978-1916415669 (cit. on p. 48).

[9] Peter G. Strasman J. H. Haynes. *Triumph 2000, 2500 and 2.5 PI Owner's Workshop Manual*. J H Haynes & Co Ltd, 1977. isbn: 978-0856963360 (cit. on p. 61).

[11] Greg Bear. *Eon*. Legend, 1987. isbn: 9780099523505 (cit. on p. 74).

Conclusion

[20] A. Einstein. "Die Grundlage der allgemeinen Relativitätstheorie". In: *Annalen der Physik* 354.7 (1916), pp. 769–822. doi: 10.1002/andp.19163540702 (cit. on p. 91).

[21] Anne-Laure Guéganic. *Louis XV: The Fastueux Order*, Éditions Atlas, Paris. 2008. isbn: 978-2-7312-3798-6 (cit. on p. 100).

[22] "X. Abstract of the results of the comparisons of the standards of length of England, France, Belgium, Prussia, Russia, India, Australia, made at the ordnance Survey Office, Southampton". In: *Philosophical Transactions of the Royal Society of London* 157 (1867), pp. 161–180. doi: 10.1098/rstl.1867.0010 (cit. on p. 101).

[23] Cassini de Thuri. *La description géométrique de la France*. l'Académie royale des sciences, 1744. url: https://catalogue.bnf.fr/ark:/12148/cb41606696m (cit. on p. 101).

[24] Sir Cornelius Vermuyden. *A discourse touching the drayning the great fennes, : lying vvithin the severall counties of Lincolne, Northampton, Huntington, Norfolke, Suffolke, Cambridge, and the isle of Ely, as it was presented to his Majestie*. London, Printed by Thomas Fawcet, dwelling in Grub-street neere the lower Pumpe, 1642, 1642 (cit. on p. 113).

[28] Ludwig Wittgenstein. *Tractatus Logico-Philosophicus*. 1921 (cit. on p. 134).

[29] Nigel Derbyshire. *Accidental Poetry: The raw conduit into my brain*. Carbon Writer, 2018. isbn: 978-1916415607 (cit. on p. 134).

[31] Douglas Adams. *The Hitchhiker's Guide to the Galaxy (42nd Anniversary Ed.)* Pan Books, 2020. isbn: 978-1529034523 (cit. on p. 155).

[34] Prospero Alpini. *De Plantis Aegypti liber*. Franciscus de Francisis, Venice, 1592. url: https : / / www . biusante . parisdescartes . fr / histoire / medica/resultats/index.php?do=livre&cote= pharma_res011987x02 (cit. on p. 174).

[35] S. Beaty-Pownall. *The "Queen" Cookery Books*. Horace Cox, London, 1902 (cit. on p. 175).

[36] Hannah Glasse. *The Art of Cookery, made Plain and Easy*. Wangford, London, 1747, p. 285 (cit. on p. 175).

[37] Robin Pogrebin. "Pineapple Pizza Tests Limits of Presidential Power in Iceland". In: *New York Times* (Feb. 22, 2017) (cit. on p. 178).

[38] In: *The Chautauquan* 3.9 (June 1, 1883). Ed. by Theodore L. Flood, p. 544 (cit. on p. 187).

TV & Movies

[10] Tim Burton (Director). *Batman*. Warner Bros. 1989 (cit. on p. 72).

[15] Ryan Fleck (Directors) Anna Boden. *Captain Marvel*. Marvel Studios. 2019 (cit. on p. 84).

[16] Joe Russo (Directors) Anthony Russo. *Avengers: Endgame*. Marvel Studios. 2019 (cit. on p. 84).

[17] Gene Roddenberry (Creator). *Star Trek: The Next Generation*. Paramount Television. 1987-1994 (cit. on p. 84).

[18] Jeri Taylor (Creators) Rick Berman Michael Piller. *Star Trek: Voyager*. Paramount Television. 1995-2001 (cit. on p. 84).

[19] J. Michael Straczynski. *Babylon 5*. Babylonian Productions. 1993-1998 (cit. on p. 84).

Conclusion

Online

[1] UK Tea & Infusions Association. *Tea Facts*. 2021. url: https://www.tea.co.uk/about-tea (visited on May 17, 2020) (cit. on p. 8).

[3] GSM Arena. *Motorola razr V3i*. 2009. url: https://www.gsmarena.com/motorola_razr_v3i-1352.php (visited on July 16, 2020) (cit. on p. 30).

[4] GSM Arena. *Nokia 7280*. 2004. url: https://www.gsmarena.com/nokia_7280-884.php (visited on July 16, 2020) (cit. on p. 30).

[12] CuriousMarc. *About Curious Marc*. 2021. url: https://www.curiousmarc.com/about (visited on May 19, 2020) (cit. on p. 78).

[13] Disney. *Disney+ Steaming*. 2021. url: https://www.disneyplus.com/ (visited on Apr. 15, 2021) (cit. on p. 83).

[14] Nick Pino. *How to watch the Marvel movies in order*. Apr. 13, 2021. url: https://www.techradar.com/how-to/how-to-watch-the-marvel-movies-in-order (visited on Apr. 15, 2021) (cit. on p. 83).

[25] Old Maps. *Old Maps Online*. 2021. url: https://www.oldmapsonline.org/ (visited on May 19, 2020) (cit. on p. 114).

[26] Nigel Derbyshire. *Author's website*. 2021. url: https://nigelderbyshire.com/ (visited on Apr. 17, 2021) (cit. on p. 118).

[27] Katherine Brooks. *There's A Japanese Word For People Who Buy More Books Than They Can Actually Read*. Apr. 23, 2017. url: https://www.huffingtonpost.co.uk/entry/theres-a-japanese-word-for-people-who-buy-more-books-than-they-can-actually-read_n_58f79b7ae4b029063d364226?ri18n=true (visited on Apr. 17, 2021) (cit. on p. 130).

Bibliography

[30] Garmin. *Garmin GPSMap 60CSx*. 2010. url: https://buy.garmin.com/en-GB/GB/p/310 (visited on Apr. 17, 2021) (cit. on p. 148).

[32] Alexander Arguelles. *Old English: Languages of the World: Introductory Overviews*. 2008. url: https://www.youtube.com/watch?v=RLJGTYkEKLI (visited on Apr. 17, 2021) (cit. on p. 167).

[33] Jenna Stoeber. *Animal Crossing's fake language sounds different in Japanese*. Polygon. Mar. 22, 2020. url: https://www.polygon.com/videos/2020/3/22/21188355/animal-crossing-new-horizons-language-video (cit. on p. 168).

[39] Instagram. *Instagram.com*. 2021. url: https://www.instagram.com (visited on Apr. 17, 2021) (cit. on p. 188).

Conclusion

About the author

Nigel Derbyshire was born in Norfolk, and currently lives somewhere else. Full of mostly true stories, he is often compelled to write them down. You will either find him sitting in a corner contemplating, or in the middle of a crowd chatting and laughing.

"Writer of words, thinker of thoughts, visions of adventure."

§

Head on over to nigelderbyshire.com to get the latest.

www.ingramcontent.com/pod-product-compliance
Lightning Source LLC
Chambersburg PA
CBHW061321040426
42444CB00011B/2724